ACQUIRING FREEDOM
FROM
FUNDAMENTALIST
RELIGIOUS THINKING

*Why and how I left Jehovah's Witnesses
after forty years*

Dieter Parczany

ACQUIRING FREEDOM FROM

FUNDAMENTALIST RELIGIOUS THINKING

Title of original edition (2014): THE FALSE TRUTH

Dieter Parczany

E-mail address for correspondence, feedback, questions:

parczany@hotmail.com

Original title in German:

Befreiung von religiöser Bevormundung

I used my pen name Peter Porjohn to publish the first
edition in 2014 and the revised edition in 2016.

Library of Congress Control Number (LCCN)
of the 2014 edition: 201 4905 142

Bible quotations are taken from the

NEW WORLD TRANSLATION

OF THE HOLY SCRIPTURES (2013 Revision)

Online edition jw.org

Grateful acknowledgement is made to

The Rev. Dr. Thomas V. Calderone

and to my wife Patricia

for editing the text of the English translation

and to Dennis Herner

for editing the text of the revised edition.

In memory of my son Manuel

who died shortly after his 8th birthday

I dedicate this book to my two daughters

Sabrina and Amelie

Comments on revised edition (2019)

I decided to publish this revised edition under my real name. Reasons to keep names and locations anonymous and to write under my pen name Peter Porjohn do not exist anymore.

Changes in the organization may appear to be huge and impressive for the individual Jehovah's Witness. In reality they are not. The organizational structures and thinking patterns are the same. There is no real organizational and spiritual renewal. This is why all information in this book is still important. I updated it according to my best knowledge in January of 2019.

Comments on revised edition (2016)

There are constant changes of organizational terms, structures and interpretation of doctrines among Jehovah's Witnesses (see especially chapters 6, 8, 10, 11, 12 and 13). This is the main reason for presenting a revised edition of my book. I also included some speculations about possible future changes and developments.

Out of consideration for people to whom I feel close and who are still Jehovah's Witnesses I have changed my name and do not mention anything which could reveal my identity.

Everything written in this book is true and has really happened.

TABLE OF CONTENTS

PROLOGUE

It was the summer of 1997. I received "the privilege" to give one of the key manuscript lectures on Sunday morning of the annual convention in Bonn for Spanish speaking Jehovah's Witnesses in Germany. I read the manuscript knowing that it is not permitted to change the text of such talks in any way, not even minor details. I knew that my conscience would never permit me to give this speech. The content was in conflict with all my acquired knowledge and I wanted to decline making the speech and send back the manuscript. But I permitted others to put me under pressure and convince me not to turn down this *privilege* despite all my concerns. I delivered the lecture with my usual enthusiasm and trained inflections and left the stage feeling nauseous. I went to the restroom and saw this pale face staring in the mirror, ready to vomit from the hypocrisy I forced my soul to commit. Everything I had done and said as a faithful, believing Jehovah's Witness, I did with sincerity and complete conviction. Now, I felt like a fraud and I could

1

not and did not want to continue living my life this way.

Religious freedom is a fundamental human right and history tells us that many people were willing to fight for it. The Constitution of the United States of America and most democratic countries protect the rights of religious freedom for a large number of denominations.

The problem is this: People defending and fighting for religious freedom usually do this to establish certain rights for their own church or organized religious group. Then, their way of practicing religion often becomes mandatory for their members. Of course, if an individual disagrees with his or her church one is free to leave. But if there is a lack of tolerance for such departures, and a rigid organizational structure exists, leaving one's religion may turn out to be a nightmare. The one wanting to escape may have a high emotional price to pay. It can affect one's health, finances, and even one's psychological well-being.

Real religious freedom should also include the right to

2

separate from a religion without threats or punishments. No one should worship in fear of disobeying rules invented or established by other human beings claiming to speak in the name of God. Everyone should have the right to think for himself and act according to his own conscience. No one's faith should be patronized by a religious organization or any group that claims to possess "*the* truth."

Faith and freedom of thought are most important values. Religious organizations insist on having the right to freely practice their own particular religion. But the one who really matters is THE INDIVIDUAL HUMAN BEING. These personal rights must be protected. Everyone who wants to liberate himself from certain religious influences should have the opportunity to do so, and get the necessary help if needed.

Institutionalized religion has a tremendous influence on the thinking and the lives of a large part of humanity. Quite a number of people are even willing to die for their religious beliefs because they have been promised a better life after death. Suicidal terrorists testify to this in a dramatic way; which is something that still shocks us each time it happens. But even on a less spectacular level, we find that millions of people are willing to die and sacrifice themselves in any number of ways for their religion.

For more than 40 years, I was influenced by Jehovah's Witnesses, a religion that claims to have "*the* truth." I hesitated to publish my story for a long time out of consideration for the feelings of my family. Several books have been published already and I didn't want to write just another book about my former religion.

In the United States of America, religious freedom exists as a fundamental right. People usually can leave their church easily or establish another one when they disagree. That is why such a wide variety of churches and religious denominations exist in this country. But this does not mean that individuals are not patronized, dominated and influenced in a way that is *damaging* (destructive to the authentic soul of a human being).

My motivation in writing this book, is to help people who are captured in all different kinds of religions. Based on my experience, I want to offer help to people who desire to break free from a dominating and damaging influence, but just don't know how to do it. Religious organizations usually have their own lawyers often defending their organizational rights in court. The individual human being who suffers from the powerful influence of a religion usually does not have the means to defend himself legally. Many of these people are in great spiritual and psychological need.

Jehovah's Witnesses claim to have "the truth." According to this belief, *all other religions* are false and belong to *"The World Empire of False Religion"* which will be destroyed shortly before Armageddon. Of course, being one of Jehovah's Witnesses is a voluntary choice; and no one will be hindered to leave. But liberating oneself from their dominating structures and beliefs requires an overwhelming struggle. Going through this experience can be truly horrific. It is an escape which may not only leave permanent emotional wounds, but inevitably brings about the loss of family and friends. For many, it is not easy to find a new spiritual home nor a new purpose in life.

But one can break free! It is possible! Acquiring personal religious freedom is spiritually and emotionally rewarding.

The message of this book is:

YOU CAN LIBERATE YOURSELF FROM A DAMAGING RELIGIOUS INFLUENCE! IT IS POSSIBLE AND THE POSITIVE RESULTS IN ONE'S PERSONAL LIFE ARE WORTH ALL THE EFFORTS!

In the second part of the book you'll find chapters 10 to 16 with information about Jehovah's Witnesses. You may find it interesting to look into it before, during or after reading my book.

I write this in memory of my son Manuel who died when he was eight years old. Due to our religious beliefs he did not receive the complete recommended treatment for his illness.

I dedicate this book to my adult daughter Sabrina who is still having a very difficult time liberating herself from the influences of her past.

I also dedicate this book to my daughter Amelie who was born in 2003. It is my desire that she will not have to go through all of those negative experiences with a religion or ideology in her own life. I want her to become a free thinking, happy human being.

I am writing this book for all who are disturbed because of being patronized by a religion or ideology. They may be in desperate need of strength and help in liberating themselves.

I am writing for all those in my extended family, my friends and acquaintances that are interested in knowing my story.

This revised edition contains updated information available to me in January of 2019. Jehovah's Witnesses will always experience changes in their organizational structures and understanding of doctrines. They are presenting it as "new light" coming from God. I have no hope that they will ever change their fundamentalist structure of thinking.

Dieter Parczany, January 2019

Chapter 1
Abuse of Power

Each one of us has the fundamental right to decide about his own life. No one should dictate to anyone else about what to think or how to live. Of course, personal freedom has its limits when it interferes with the rights and the well-being of others. I am sure that most would agree with these fundamental statements.

The abuse of power is a widespread problem despite these fundamental rights. In one way or another, most of us have experienced the suffering that originates from the abuse of power. Maybe our parents had outbursts of anger or disciplined us physically, or maybe we were threatened by "stronger" children or teenagers in the schoolyard, or had to suffer the injustices of a teacher or a boss who lacked self-control. The list could be continued.

But a much more severe abuse of power exists. This book directs the attention to what can occur under the auspices of religion.

There are people who claim to be spokesmen of God, to be his "channel" which He uses to reveal His will for all people. They say that their religion is the only true one. These people believe that they have divine authorization to publish rules for everyday life, to supervise and judge others. If this would really be true, then defying those men in control would be like standing up against God.

What higher authority could one have than claiming to speak in God's name being His "channel of revelation"? Imagine belonging to a group of people with which God deals exclusively, revealing to only the few chosen, His spiritual light and understanding about His purpose and will!

It is a sad fact that the lives of millions of people are controlled, dominated and influenced in this way. This has consequences on how they spend their time and their money. It affects their plans for life, including decisions about what career they choose, whether they should get married, stay single, or whether or not to have children. It has an effect on their emotional and physical health. They are told what kind of medical treatment or medication is acceptable or unacceptable to God. People are even willing to go to prison or die for a God who reveals Himself through human beings as they are made to believe.

This is not right and it is dangerous! The claim of knowing what God thinks is something presumptuous. It is also presumptuous to declare that God reveals His knowledge to human beings who are claiming to be His representatives. Nobody has a God given right to tell others what to think and how to act. The claim to have "*the* truth" is a lie!

But it is a sad fact and I can testify to it that people are turning with great faithfulness and confidence to such "earthly representatives" of God or to "His organization." They inquire about God's viewpoint on behavior and conduct in practically every situation of everyday life; even the most intimate of matters and direct these questions to "God's organization."

Here are just a few examples that come to my mind:
Is standing up when a national anthem is played or saluting a flag really idolatry in God's eyes? Does God condemn the actual standing up or does the idolatrous act begin with putting one's hand on the heart?
Is it correct for a Christian man with responsibilities in church to wear a mustache or a beard?
How long should the skirt of a Christian woman be? Above the knee, in the middle of the knee or should it cover the knee?
Is it appropriate for a woman to wear slacks in church?
Are you worshiping the God of Luck when you play lotto?
Should a Christian work at a cash register where cigarettes are sold?

Do not think that the list stops here. I could go on with an endless catalogue of ridiculous questions. All kinds of questions are submitted to these men, who say that they represent God's organization. They feel authorized by God to make decisions defining appropriate Christian conduct in every aspect of life.

People expect God's answer through His channel of earthly representatives even about the most intimate details in life.

What sexual practices are permitted for a married couple? May two people who love each other but are not married yet, hold hands or kiss? Where are they permitted to touch each other?

What kind of behavior is a reason for separation or divorce? What kind of treatment by one's spouse is considered to be tolerable?

Does God condemn masturbation?

A so-called "Governing Body" made up of a few "old" men, in the past some of them being unmarried, have no scruples to answer in God's name creating unbelievable consequences for many, many people.

But the abuse of power goes even further. Answers concerning questions of faith and conduct are given in an *anonymous* way! Members of "God's organization" are writing articles, books and letters to individuals without signature or mentioning the name of the one writing. God's organization or His church is answering as if God Himself is speaking.

Is there a greater abuse of power than this?

Of course there is the declaration that the organization is not infallible, not inspired by God. But in reality obedience is expected for the instructions by "God's Organization." If one wants to continue to be in good standing, one has to believe in "the truth" as it is revealed under the guidance of God's Spirit in all publications and letters.

Albert Einstein once said: "Few are those who see with their own eyes and feel with their own hearts."

I am writing this book with the intention to offer some help to people who are in religious or ideological "captivity." Captive because they are lacking the development of their true self. Captive as they do not see with their own eyes or feel with their own hearts. They may empower or permit

14

others to see and feel for them. Some may even think that it is a sin to think for themselves or to decide for themselves. They want to submit humbly to God, but in reality they are allowing their fellow human beings to exercise power over them.

This is my message to sincere but mislead victims of organized religion:

The fear to lose God's favor is unfounded. This fear is only a man-made weapon to control people! You are not rebelling against God just because you do not agree with what people want to make you believe and do. You do not have to be afraid of God's punishment because of not obeying rules made up by self-appointed representatives of God.

Chapter 2

Background and motives

I was born into a religious environment of Jehovah's Witnesses and my life was completely shaped and influenced accordingly. It effected my way of thinking, feeling and acting; my goals in life were shaped by my faith. Today I am happy and very grateful that I was able to escape from this influence and to recognize and change dangerous thinking patterns. I was also able to cope successfully with the emotional damage done to me. In the second part of my life, I was able to enjoy a new beginning; being free from any spiritual dictatorship, I am open-minded to new thoughts and new spiritual paths.

How was it possible to liberate myself from such a spiritual prison? THE KEY WAS TO GATHER FACTS AND TO RE-EXAMINE MY BELIEFS over a period of years. I was able to change my viewpoint on doctrines and interpretations as well as rules and patterns of conduct by obtaining knowledge. I then recognized that certain beliefs

16

and rules were just not true; they do not agree with the facts. The so-called "TRUTH" is not true. This helped me to escape from religious bondage without being haunted with a bad conscience. Despite disagreeing with the doctrines and leaving my religion, I do *not* fear divine punishment.

In telling my story, it is my goal not to blame particular individuals in this religious organization. I have known many people personally who serve on the highest organizational level of Jehovah's Witnesses and have enjoyed some very close friendships. My opinion is that these religious leaders are victims themselves, often not conscious about the effects their decisions have on people.

They are just not able or willing to see certain things. Not one of my former friends or religious brothers and sisters was able or willing to answer my questions and respond to my doubts. Maybe they were unconsciously afraid to confront themselves with my thoughts. There is a fear that comes when one questions THE TRUTH. What happens if there is proof that THE TRUTH is not true?

It wasn't until I was 45 years old that I felt able to liberate myself from religious oppression. Why did it take so long? Why did it take an additional fifteen years for me to start writing my story?

I will attempt to describe my spiritual development. Although I was one of Jehovah's Witnesses, my comments do not only reflect this particular religious group, but any religious or political structure patronizing people. Although I am relating my own specific experience, I want others to understand the principal application of my conclusions to any religious or spiritual captivity. I am convinced that institutionalized or organized religion in itself holds many dangers. If one wants to be close to God one does not need a church, an organization or a community. It is possible for you and me to find our own spiritual way and happiness outside of any organization.

Sociologist Eric Hoffer offered sufficient scientific evidence that similar structures exist in all religious organizations and political parties. His book *The True Believer* shows clearly that many people are patronized by all different kind of organizations. This of course differs according to strictness of authority and willingness to be tolerant toward one's own members.

Despite those facts I do not deny that much good has been provided by organized religion. Some religious groups offer a haven with a less judgmental atmosphere for believers who are seeking community with others. Some people seem to need a sense of security and community which they find in religious denominations. Belonging to a religious brotherhood or sisterhood gives meaning to the lives of many.

Observing different religions I have seen tolerance where I least expected it. I once attended a lecture of a high ranking Catholic bishop in Germany, followed by a question and answer period. An audience member asked his opinion about a prominent Catholic theologian who had attacked the pope, the Vatican and Catholic doctrines in many of his books and in public. The bishop responded

19

that a large Christian church has to be able to cope with such a person, to tolerate him and to listen to his criticism.

There is a danger to underestimate the harmful influence of Christian fundamentalist religions.

Jehovah's Witnesses are peaceful people. They do not approve of violence, political revolutions or any terrorist activities. They are nice, honest and sincere people. Their ministers are usually kind and humorous. Nobody exploits them financially. No one of their "leaders" lives in luxury. They help each other in good and bad times.

On the other hand, fundamentalist thinking has a strong influence even in most private and intimate aspects of their lives. They are living in a "bubble." Jehovah's Witnesses are convinced that only they have THE TRUTH. According to their beliefs all other human systems, all governments of the world, all other religions are under the influence of Satan, the Devil. They believe that all will be destroyed by Jesus and his angels in the expected "great tribulation" culminating in Armageddon. Jehovah's Witnesses are willing to die, to go to prison, to leave and to shun their friends and family members if this is required by the current Bible interpretation of the "Governing Body" of their organization.

Chapter 3

The key to spiritual liberation

KNOWLEDGE is the ultimate key for a successful escape from spiritual bondage. How can one use this key and obtain necessary knowledge about facts? I recommend two things, which have helped me in my situation:

HAVE THE COURAGE TO CONTRADICT
YOUR BELIEFS!
QUESTION THE TRUTHFULNESS
OF WHAT YOUR WERE TAUGHT!

COMPARE AND ANALYSE THE REASONING AND EVIDENCE WHICH PEOPLE ARRIVING AT DIFFERENT CONCLUSIONS PRESENT.

These two recommendations sound simple. Easily one may not take them serious enough and not apply them.

22

It is a huge step and much courage is necessary to question the truthfulness of one's own convictions, beliefs of one's parents and teachings of one's religion! *The truth* should be able to face and give answers to a critical exam.

Valuable tools such as encyclopedias, dictionaries, alternative Bible translations and commentaries are good sources. There is a large quantity of controversial literature about almost every question and subject. All of this is easily accessible in libraries and bookstores. Of course much information can be obtained through the internet.

Naturally people have different opinions and beliefs but, I would ask, are all people who do not belong to my religion Christians without sincere motives? Is everyone else who believes differently ignorant or spiritually blind? For people who think that one's own religion is the only true religion, it may come as a surprise to find out that there are many sincere and intelligent "seekers of truth" every-where, inside and outside of religious denominations.

Why do many of my former religious brothers and sisters

suffer so much emotionally after leaving the organization of Jehovah's Witnesses? Many leave because they are disappointed by other human beings and have suffered because of the way they were treated. Many were "disfellowshipped" or excommunicated by so-called "judicial committees" because of "conduct unbecoming of a Christian" as it is defined by this religion. Many have been suffering emotionally and spiritually for years and they are torn between a bad conscience and an incapability to meet certain requirements or moral standards. They might have doubts, but still believe they were taught "the truth" about Jehovah, the Bible and many of its teachings. It may be difficult for many to forget their negative personal experiences. This is why most published books about Jehovah's Witnesses contain life stories and personal experiences made in this organization. Many started considering the truthfulness of doctrines only *after* they went through negative personal experiences and disappointments. Their emotional wounds hurt for a long time.

I am convinced that the key for successful liberation out

of religious bondage is knowledge. Question whether certain viewpoints and doctrines really are true. Does the list of rules about acceptable or improper behavior really reflect God's thoughts, or is it defined and explained by humans in the name of God? This examination is very important! Knowing facts can be an eye opener and the key to liberating oneself from unnecessary guilt feelings. If God does not condemn a certain conduct, or if certain doctrines or dogmas are just not true, one does not have to have a bad conscience or fear divine punishment. KNOWLEDGE IS THE KEY.

I was tempted to write a theological book about the interpretation of Bible scriptures by Jehovah's Witnesses and why they cannot be correct. I did not because everyone must find his own way. Each person has the right to arrive at different conclusions and results and find their own "truth."

Once, I was convinced "to be in the truth" or "to have the truth." Never again will I claim to know all the right answers. I want to keep my mind open for facts and ways

25

of reasoning unknown to me today. With certainty I do know that things which I believed in the past cannot be true. I am happy that I was able to free myself from *spiritual chains*. I can live contented with the existence of question marks in my life. I refuse to be influenced again by false "truths", lies, false interpretations and dogmas which only damage the human soul.

The problem of "truth finding" can be illustrated very well in a little story which I read some time ago. I have changed the story for the purpose of this book. It is titled:

"The Truth Store"

Once I saw a store with a sign "Selling Truth." I entered with the wish to buy truth.

A salesman welcomed me saying: "What kind of Truth do you want to buy?"

"What do you have and how much does Truth cost?" I asked.

"Well, each Truth has its price. We are offering: Half-

Truth, Fictitious-Truth, Temporary-Truth, Tranquilizing-Truth, Changing-Truth, Latest-Truth, Simple-Truth, Complicated-Truth and Painful-Truth."

"No, no", I said, "I want to buy the whole, the real truth, 'THE TRUTH', so to speak. Is it available and what does it cost?"

"Yes, we have it, but it is very expensive, there is no discounted offer. It may cost you a temporary loss of peace of mind and heart, a possible loss of relatives and friends, sleepless nights, possible panic attacks, insecurity, more question marks than answers, an uncertain future and no guarantees. Do you really want to pay this price? . . ."

I am convinced that it is worthwhile to pay that price for spiritual freedom. Never again shall I be patronized by a religious organization or any kind of ideology or philosophy. I will no longer allow anyone to control my thinking or limit my freedom to question anything. But I know that some people are different; they prefer to be "a happy prisoner", afraid of freedom with all its insecurities, options and dangers.

Chapter 4

Why do people stay in a religion?

Why do people hesitate to examine the truthfulness of their religion?

Why do people stay in a religion although they disagree with what is taught and done in their church?

Why do most men in responsible positions of such a religion stay faithful, defending their organization's teachings and procedures although they know better?

Here are a few reasons that apply to Jehovah's Witnesses. Some of these reasons can also be applied to other religious and political systems.

Simple answers to complicated questions of life may give a certain feeling of security. Knowing all the answers contributes to the feeling of having "the truth." Intelligent minds have been searching for answers about life and death and the world we live in for thousands of years. Being able to give simple answers to complicated questions is considered to be a proof that one belongs to the only true religion.

One does *not have to deal with one's own mortality* if one believes that real life begins after the resurrection of the dead. It doesn't matter how much one suffers, or how much one sacrifices oneself, or how little joy one has, there will be a reward after the resurrection and all negative experiences will be forgotten. If one wants to see his dead loved ones again, one has to stick faithfully to the only true religion. Life everlasting is promised only to all those who do not lose God's blessings.

Some people feel the need to belong to the only *worldwide brotherhood* with sincere, honest, and peaceful happy people. A high-ranking representative of Jehovah's Witnesses once told me after being at a social gathering: "The existence of this brotherhood alone makes it worthwhile to be part of our organization, even if everything we believe and teach would be false."

Staying a believing member of a religion may help to

maintain *a calm conscience*. One may feel that one can have a good conscience living up to the divine rules as they are understood and explained by God's earthly channel. If one "sins" one can easily get God's forgiveness: Personal prayer or confession to the elders of the congregation in case of "severe" sins guarantees God's forgiveness.

Some are convinced that there is *no alternative* to the only true religion. Very frequently the apostle Peter is quoted saying to Jesus: "Where shall we go? You have words of everlasting life" (John 6:68). Falsely interpreted and taken out of the context, this Bible quote is used to say: "To what other religion do you want to go? Our organization is unique in this world. Where else can you find such a brotherhood and such an understanding of truth?" One easily accepts such reasoning, especially if one is not prepared to mention a list of *better* religions or a number of alternative possibilities and explanations. To justify the imperfections of their organization one gets reminded about conditions in the early Christian church or for example the ancient people of Israel and how they were still God's people despite their imperfections.

30

Calling themselves "Jehovah's Witnesses" is evidence enough for many that they belong to God's people, the only true religion. Several Bible scriptures concerning *the name "Jehovah"* are misinterpreted to prove this. For example:

"YOU are my witnesses," is the utterance of Jehovah, "even my servant whom I have chosen, in order that YOU may know and have faith in me, and that YOU may understand that I am the same One." (Isaiah 43:10) or:

"For everyone who calls on the name of Jehovah will be saved." (Romans 10:13) or:

"Sym'eon · on has related thoroughly how God for the first time turned his attention to the nations to take out of them a people for his name" (Acts 15:14).

There are still more excuses for not leaving a patronizing religion, all of which are based on fear. They include:

Fear to be unfaithful to the *religion of one's parents.*

Fear to lose one's *spouse and family*, or make them suffer.

Fear of *being alone* because of losing all friends and social contacts.

Fear that something could be true about "the truth" and that "Armageddon" or "*Judgment Day*" does come after all and one would lose the prospects of everlasting life.

Fear of losing *one's stability in life* by becoming a victim of all different kinds of addictions.

Fear of *losing self-esteem*, which was obtained by enjoying certain positions or "privileges" in one's church. This could be especially true if one experienced a certain degree of attention, respect and honor.

Fear to *lose material security* and provisions of health care. This especially applies to people who work at the headquarters and branches of my former religion. For example, people who were dismissed because of disagreeing with the organization had difficulties finding a new job and health insurance especially when they were already older.

Why do most men in responsible positions of such a religion stay faithful to their organization and beliefs although they know better? Well, despite their insight and knowledge they may really believe that God guides and blesses them in his earthly organization. Another aspect, although they may not admit this, may be the importance of their position, the honor, attention and material benefits they receive. In chapter 12 of this book you can find some information about the topic "Jehovah's Witnesses and money."

Even though they have been patronized and their lives have been negatively influenced, there are many reasons which make people stay in a religion.

For my part I am happy to be free. I prefer to be like the seagull in Richard Bach's book *Jonathan Livingston*

Seagull, the one who enjoyed experimenting flying freely against the rules of the flock. I wholeheartedly recommend reading it, for it served as a great encouragement to me. In like manner, I found Hermann Hesse's book *Siddhartha* to be very helpful. In it Hesse describes the ways of a truth seeking man in the Asiatic world. These books and their adaptations to movies can be of great help and encouragement to people who want to liberate themselves from religious or political bondage.

One man who was able to break free was Raymond Franz. As a former member of the "Governing Body" of Jehovah's Witnesses, his familiarity with the highest level of hierarchy in this organization was unparalleled. He was already advanced in age when he spiritually liberated himself from his religion. Franz is the author of *Crisis of Conscience* and *The Search of Christian Freedom*, two books I recommend as required reading to all Jehovah's Witnesses who want to get more information and insight about their religion and how it works. These publications, supported as they are by sound reasoning and a representation of facts without bitter accusation, help to

34

explain why certain passages of the Bible as interpreted by Jehovah's Witnesses cannot be correct.

With this in mind, let me say that it is not my intention to criticize or condemn people who come to different conclusions than I. Everyone has the right to believe, to live and to die as they choose. Yet, I think it needs to be acknowledged that while some people are more adept at facing life's challenges, others are happy to live in a "fictitious" world. It reminds me of the psychiatrist who once said of some of his patients that lived in an unreal dream world: "Some are so happy that I wonder if I really would like to cure them if I could." By no means do I want to judge people who feel happy and secure in an unreal world. I only want to offer help to people who want to liberate themselves and tell them that it is possible, it can be done!

Chapter 5

How my religion affected my life for forty years

This chapter may not fulfill the expectations of some readers. I served in many different capacities in the organization of Jehovah's Witnesses. I know people personally who are or were on the highest organizational level of responsibility. I am familiar with the organizational structures and have gained insight into many procedures not known to the average Witness. I could fill a book with negative experiences, revealing such internal and confidential information, but this is not the purpose of my book. I want to demonstrate with my story how, for over 40 years, my thinking and my life had been shaped and how it was possible to liberate myself little by little from this spiritual captivity.

Religious influence during my childhood

Through the influence of my parents, I believed in the existence of God from my earliest childhood. I believed that God was watching me and blessing me when I asked for His guidance and help. I always imagined Him as a loving and merciful God who is patient and willing to forgive our sins and help us. We expected "the end of the world", but I was never afraid about it, nor had I ever feared His punishment.

As long as I can remember our family attended religious meetings and services three times a week. Three times a year we also went to large assemblies which lasted several days. They were willing to make every effort and go any distance. My parents really took their faith seriously, the only reason for missing a religious service was illness. As a small child I accompanied my father in door to door evangelizing work, preaching "the good news of God's kingdom." I was impressed with his knowledge of the Bible. When he opened the Bible and quoted from it, nobody was really able to respond.

When I was eight years old I got "the privilege" to read the first chapter of The Book of Job in front of an audience in our "Kingdom Hall" (church building) in Tuttlingen, Germany. We had a Bible (Elberfelder Translation) with old fashioned letters, which were difficult to read. Therefore my father wrote the whole chapter on a typewriter to make it easier for me to read. This was an early and small beginning of my career as preacher and speaker.

Later in life, as my responsibility grew, I presided at religious services, giving sermons three or more times per week in German, English, Spanish and Greek (mostly with help of an interpreter). I lectured in many different locations to audiences from 20 to 40,000 people. According to my own estimate I lectured or presided at religious services four thousand to four and a half thousand times in my life. During the 1970's and 1980's I became very well known among Jehovah's Witnesses. Therefore, many were shocked when I left the organization and it was not possible for me to withdraw in a silent way, as I had planned.

Impressive childhood memories of the 1950's were visits in our home from survivors of the NAZI concentration camps of Adolf Hitler. Many had been imprisoned for many years because of their faith. My parents were very hospitable and we frequently had guests in our home. During this time we heard many stories of their wartime experiences, the years suffering in concentration camps and of how some of our brothers suffered unnecessary deaths.

There were those who interpreted certain rules from God's organization more strictly than others. For example: Could a Christian put hay on a wagon which was destined for a military camp? Should someone put his life in danger smuggling or copying Watchtower articles (magazine of Jehovah's Witnesses)? Answers to such questions could decide between life and death.

I grew up in the small town Spaichingen in the Southern

part of Germany that was mostly Catholic. Naturally we were considered outsiders, as we neither attended church, celebrated Christmas nor participated in other Catholic holidays. Likewise there were no birthday celebrations. But I do not remember my parents being religious fanatics; and to my recollection I never really suffered from being different. My parents saw to it that we had all joys of a childhood. And of course, we were convinced that we belonged to the true religion, that we had God's blessing and prospects of everlasting life "in an earthly paradise."

Still, Jehovah's Witnesses did encourage parents to discipline their children physically. Once in a while we got beaten with a belt or stick by my father, but this was an experience of many children growing up in the 1950's.

Being very balanced, my parents did not isolate me from so called "unbelievers." I was permitted to play with the neighborhood children Catholic or Protestant. I was not, however, permitted to join any club, though my parents did tolerate my craziness for soccer as well as table tennis, bike racing, swimming, climbing trees, playing the accordion and other activities that were important for a little boy.

Decisions during my teenager years

When we moved to Berlin, Germany in 1964 I was 12 years old and starting to make decisions concerning religious life. At the age of 13 years, convinced I had sufficient religious knowledge to make a concrete decision, I dedicated my life to Jehovah God in prayer and declared this publicly at a convention of Jehovah's Witnesses by water baptism. I wanted to follow Christ wholeheartedly and serve God with all my time and energy. Because of my willingness to volunteer in all different kinds of church activities, I received certain "privileges" and responsibilities in our congregation at a very young age. By the age of 16, I became a fulltime minister or "Pioneer" and was participating in our evangelizing work more than 100 hours per month. Additionally, I presided in bible study groups and gave sermons in our congregation.

Of course all this was motivated by my love and dedication to God and being convinced that I was a part of the only true religion. But there was another reason that possessed me to be so active. Over the protests of my teachers, I quit High School after 9th grade, convinced as I was that the "end of the world" or "Armageddon" was near, almost "at hand."

Let me explain more fully the rational for my thinking. Chapter 24 of the Gospel of Matthew relates how Jesus was talking about the sign of His Second Coming. He is quoted saying: "Truly I say to YOU, that this generation will by no means pass away until all these things occur" (Verse 34). "God's organization" interpreted for us the significance and meaning of these words: Some of the people who were old enough to observe the outbreak of World War I in 1914, the beginning of "the last days" would still be alive when the "end of the world" (Armageddon) would come. Faithful Christians (i.e. "faithful Jehovah's Witnesses") would survive Armageddon and continue to live forever in a Paradise on earth under the Millennium reign of Jesus Christ.

Since the book of Psalms declared the average of a human

life span is about 70 to 80 years the "end" really had to be close. Additionally, we were told in 1966 that according to Bible chronology 6,000 years of human history since Adam's creation would end in October of 1975. In 1968 the book *The Truth that leads to Eternal Life* (called in short "Truth-Book" by Jehovah's Witnesses) was published. In this book Dean Acheson, former United States Secretary of State was quoted saying in 1960 that he had enough information to state that the world would be too dangerous to live in within fifteen years (by 1975). Jehovah's Witnesses were proud to say that their "Truth-Book" was one of the most widely distributed books worldwide after the Bible, although it is not used nor available anymore.

Believing this, how could someone spend his time and life better than participating in spreading and preaching "this good news of God's kingdom"? We believed that this evangelizing work was saving lives. Based on the individual's reaction to our preaching work people were separated into "goats and sheep" and would receive everlasting life or suffer eternal death according to God's judgment. In the meantime Jehovah's Witnesses have changed their understanding and explanation of Jesus' parable about "the separation of goats and sheep" according to Matthew 25:31-46.

In 1971, at the age of 19, I received the "privilege" of becoming a "Special Pioneer", i.e. a fulltime minister receiving special assignments by the supervising Branch Office in Germany. I was evangelizing at least 150 hours a month. Additionally, I had responsibilities in congregations with specific needs and problems. At this time we were not covered by any health insurance (which is different now, at least in some countries). After having reported that we really did preach at least 150 hours, we received a very small monthly allowance. It was so little that my parents and other members of our church supported me financially so that I could pay my rent and living expenses.

During my life as an adult

In spring of 1974 I received an invitation to attend the Watchtower Bible School of Gilead in New York, at the headquarters of Jehovah's Witnesses. This was considered an extraordinary privilege. I was 22 years old and had already accumulated some experience in all existing positions within a local congregation. Having excellent recommendations, I was one out of 25 people selected from all over the world for the class in 1974. "Gilead" is a missionary school, but in reality an "elite group" would be trained under the direct supervision of the "Governing Body" of Jehovah's Witnesses. Here it is determined how and in what capacities the organization will use people whom they know personally. In this way a worldwide hierarchy network is created.

During this time I obtained insights and knowledge not accessible to the average Jehovah's Witness. I was able to talk to people on the highest level of this organization and developed personal relationships and even close

46

friendships. Robert Wallen (secretary of the Watchtower's president N.H. Knorr for many decades) and his wife Lorraine viewed me as their "own son." Both have passed away by now. Even in later years I spent vacation periods with the Wallens and with Gene Smalley (helper to the Governing Body and one of the senior writers of the Watchtower) and his wife Anita (who originally was from Berlin).

Additionally, there were opportunities for countless "open" conversations which are only possible among insiders on this level. As long as the person you talk to is convinced of your loyalty, you could express thoughts and questions for which common followers might be excommunicated. As long as you were faithful to the organization, it is the only level where one is permitted to question or doubt the truthfulness of certain doctrines or procedures.

I completed this training receiving good grades, a diploma, and best recommendations. During the next five years I worked in the Branch Office of Spain in Barcelona and in

Zaragoza and Valencia in my missionary assignment. I lived there as an illegal resident as the government under General Franco did not give visas to missionaries of Jehovah's Witnesses in those years. I had to learn a new language, but I loved the country and the mentality of the people. I gave lectures in front of small and large audiences, once even in a large bull fight arena filled with thousands of enthusiastic families. I enjoyed many friendships which all ended after I left the religion. I couldn't believe that people only liked me because I was one of Jehovah's Witnesses.

In 1977 I got married to a "Special Pioneer." When my wife Gabriele became pregnant, I had to give up my missionary status and quit my activity as a full time minister. Returning to my home country Germany I was faced with the challenge of providing for my family, as a high school dropout, having no profession. I got a job working for the Post office distributing mail and telegrams for several years. In my spare time I continued to be active as an "elder" in different congregations of Berlin, giving lectures at assemblies and local congregations. I was also appointed to serve as a member on several organizational committees.

At this time our religion was banned in the GDR (German Democratic Republic). I was used by the Watchtower Society as a secret undercover agent smuggling microfilms and secret information for Jehovah's Witnesses. My contact person was Wolfgang Meise, a member of the underground working branch committee in the GDR. Despite being a father of two small children, I was willing to risk my freedom.

My continued intensive Bible study and reading, and my growing insight into the organizational structures of Jehovah's Witnesses contributed to many doubts and unanswered questions. However, I never doubted fundamental things and continued to be convinced that we had "the truth" and that I belonged to the "only true religion" recognized and used by God. I kept telling myself, human errors and a lack of correct understanding also existed in the early Christian church and by the people of ancient Israel. One had to wait patiently and humble himself until God revealed further understanding. And where else should I go, to whom should I turn? There was obviously no alternative to our unique worldwide brotherhood - or was there?

Chapter 6

Liberating myself after 40 years

A spiritual turning point

A "new understanding" about "the generation" in Matthew 24 was published in The Watchtower of November 1, 1995. A completely different definition of the term "generation" was given. Now the new "understanding revealed under God's spirit" was the same understanding other religious groups had had for centuries! I could not believe what I was reading in The Watchtower magazine. The "generation" which wasn't supposed to pass away before the end of the world, did not exist anymore. The way of reasoning was unbelievable. I felt betrayed and wrote to my friends Robert and Lorraine Wallen at the headquarters in New York. Their answers were a great disappointment and completely unsatisfactory. They basically just admonished me to be faithful to God's organization.

Thanks to the computer and a CD containing most publications of the Watchtower Society, I was able to print every single comment in Watchtower publications about "this generation" in Matthew 24. I found hundreds of comments published since 1950, before 1950 this scripture was never really mentioned or even commented upon. The results of my research were absolutely clear. It was not just a matter of an interpretation of a scripture or of a *possible* understanding of Jesus' words. Jehovah's Witnesses were convinced that God's Spirit revealed to them the understanding of the 1914 generation, which would not pass away until the end. Now it was claimed that the new understanding about this generation also came about under the guidance of God's Holy Spirit.

The basic motivation for my dedicated life as a Jehovah's Witness was my love for God. But factors which affected my life planning was the conviction that "the end" was near and the generation of 1914 would not pass away till "the end of the world" would come. I quit school after 9th grade, I did not learn a trade or had a profession, I did not make any plans or provisions for retirement age – all this because I was convinced that we were living in the "last days" and that the second coming of Christ was very close.

I felt betrayed and asked myself whether I hadn't been a victim of more misleading, false and damaging interpretations of The Bible. If Jehovah's Witnesses really had "the truth", their doctrines should be able to pass a critical examination.

Didn't I have the Bible's promise that if I ask God for wisdom it would be given to me?

James 1:5 says: "So, if any one of YOU is lacking in wisdom, let him keep on asking God, for he gives generously to all and without reproaching; and it will be given him."

Jesus says according to Matthew 7:7-11: "Keep on asking, and it will be given YOU; keep on seeking, and YOU will find; keep on knocking, and it will be opened to YOU. For everyone asking receives, and everyone seeking finds, and to everyone knocking it will be opened. Indeed, who is the man among YOU whom his son asks for bread—he will not hand him a stone, will he? Or, perhaps, he will ask for a fish—he will not hand him a serpent, will he? Therefore, if YOU, although being wicked, know how to give good gifts to YOUR children, how much more so will YOUR Father who is in the heavens give good things to those asking him?"

I decided to put this promise of God to test during a period of 1,000 hours of study. I started to read The Bible again and reexamine my understanding of Bible teachings for one entire year, three hours a day.

During this year I prayed for divine wisdom daily, sometimes intensively with tears. I even temporarily considered whether somehow I had become a victim of Satan's influence. Although I had read the entire Bible before several times in my life, I did it again using different translations, as well as Interlinear Bibles and dictionaries in Hebrew and Greek. Important parts of the

54

New Testament I re-read and studied repeatedly. I examined how different Bible commentators understood certain scriptures and parts of The Bible and why.

The results were overwhelmingly clear. I recognized the wrong reasoning and false interpretation of all doctrines as they were explained by my religion. What I had considered "the truth" till then was simply false and did not agree with the facts.

The bad thing about this was not the fact that our religion interpreted and understood Bible doctrines differently than others did, but that it became more and more obvious to me what a damaging influence this had on people. A false understanding, a false interpretation of biblical text scriptures was used to influence in a most detailed and intimate way, the lives of millions of people following this religion. As a result of this people were even willing to die. People lost spouses, children, parents and friends; people lost their jobs, they suffered economic loss; some even unnecessarily were imprisoned for many years; people became ill physically, psychologically, suffering depression; and in some cases committing suicide. And all this just because of a particular interpretation of Scripture, an understanding which could change under the "guidance of God's Spirit" at any time! These were all rules and guidelines published by men who claimed to be "God's earthly channel" having a tremendous influence on people's lives.

It is true, that past mistakes and the necessity for changes had been admitted. But there was never a personal apology to people who suffered because of an "old" (false) understanding. Unless forced by court decisions there was no rehabilitation or compensation, the counsel was given to humbly accept God's discipline and to be obedient and patient.

However, given everything mentioned, I do not believe that the responsible men intentionally want to harm and deceive people. They are victims of this religious system themselves. Primarily because mostly, they really believe what they say and write.

The question then becomes, why do they respond aggressively and harshly to "apostates" who were their former brothers and friends? It would seem logical that if they were confident about having "the truth", then they should be able to respond in a friendly and patient manner showing better arguments and reasoning. They truly believe that they are doing the proper thing in the eyes of God and that they can protect themselves and their organization by excommunicating people who think differently. In reality, they must feel insecure being unable to present convincing arguments against certain objections, questions and doubts directed to them.

Meanwhile the direction I wanted and had to go was clear to myself. I had to separate from this religion if I did not want to be a hypocrite and if I didn't want to become spiritually and psychologically ill. During this process of separation, I tried to keep as honest as I possibly could while carrying out responsibilities in the congregation. For example, I only talked about selected topics in a way that my conscience would permit. In addition to deviating from certain procedures and instructions of the organization, attempting to do it in a way others would not notice, I tried to delegate certain responsibilities and limited my activity on certain committees.

Though I was conscious about how fast, harsh and merciless the reaction to my doubts or signs of my unfaithfulness would be, I was not about to allow them to excommunicate me as an "apostate." Taking the feelings of my family into consideration I wanted to find my own personal way of separating. I will relate just one example to illustrate how such mechanisms and procedures in this religion work.

An example of religious non-tolerance

For many years Jehovah's Witnesses distributed a booklet for school children and their teachers, which explained what is unacceptable for Jehovah's Witnesses during their school time. For example, they were not to participate in elections for the student body. The reasoning being that Jesus was not active politically and that He refused it when people tried to make Him king.

Jehovah's Witnesses reject the system of democracy as they believe in a theocracy, where everything is determined by God. Their basic belief is that political systems are under Satan's influence as he is the "God of that world", that will all be destroyed in Armageddon by God's kingdom. This is why Jehovah's Witnesses do not participate in politics nor do they accept political positions. This is also the reason why they refuse military service; they are not willing to become part of a military organization even if it would only include a civil duty or working in a humanitarian program.

On one occasion I was discussing our "School-Booklet" with Gene Smalley, a senior member of the writing staff of the Watchtower Society, commenting on its lack of Biblical evidence for many of the rules. To my surprise he was very conscious about the issues and problems related to the "School-Booklet" and indicated that there would be a change. In effect, one year later a new booklet was published with a completely different outline. Many of those non-Bible based rules were not mentioned again, including one concerning the election of class president. Consequently, I agreed that my daughter could participate in the next round of elections in her school.

In our congregation it was my assignment to talk about the new "School-Booklet" during our church service. I did this with enthusiasm, of course also citing that the issue of participation in class elections was no longer mentioned.

This disturbed Friedhelm Kroll, a conservative thinking co-elder of our congregation and without speaking to me about it, he filed a complaint with our Branch Office.

60

Shortly thereafter a hostile notice arrived stating that Jehovah's Witnesses still do not participate in student elections of any kind and if my daughter does not agree with this she will be denied privileges within the congregation.

In response, I wrote a letter to our Branch Office asking for an explanation. Up to this point the revised, or new publication, was always considered "new light" as it replaced the old publication. I asked whether this is different in the case of the "School-Booklet." I also mentioned that when Jesus lived, no democratic elections existed. He withdrew when people tried to appoint him to be their king. On the other hand majority votes are used to decide issues in the Governing Body and other committees in our organization.

I never directly received a response. The answer came in a letter to our body of elders threatening that if I did not change my attitude and opinion I would lose all my privileges in the congregation. There was no effort to answer my questions, only a repetition of phrases and lecturing me on loyalty to God's organization. I was willing to give in and stated publicly in front of the congregation that my comments about class elections were not correct. Coincidentally, for a certain period of time I did not receive any privileges of lecturing at big assemblies, although no explanations were given to me.

Sometime later, during the last seminar for elders that I attended, a statement was read from the Governing Body of Jehovah's Witnesses informing that everyone could decide as to whether or not they want to participate in class elections as long as it is not a direct political election. This decision has never been published in The Watchtower or any other publication. Furthermore, there was a letter to the body of elders of all congregations with instructions to destroy all remaining copies of the old "School-Booklet."

My decision

Family members and friends urged me not to make a fast decision. They asked me to give God's Spirit a chance to help me get back on the right path by waiting for the big annual assembly and by attending the special seminar for elders in January of 1998. I agreed although this meant a time of spiritual suffering for me. Here are two examples during those most difficult months in my life.

The first began in the summer of 1997 when I received "the privilege" to give one of the key manuscript lectures on the Sunday morning of our big annual convention. It is not permitted to change the text of the manuscript of such talks in any way, not even in the little details. Behind the stage there is always someone in the office assigned to simultaneously follow along in the manuscript while it is delivered as a speech to the audience. This way it is guaranteed that the same special information is communicated to the brotherhood worldwide. It is considered a great honor (the *privileges* they speak about) to present such a lecture.

I read the manuscript and I knew that my conscience would never permit me to give this speech. The contents were in conflict with all my acquired knowledge and I wanted to decline making the speech and send back the manuscript. In the end I gave into peer pressure of those who convinced me not to turn down this *privilege* despite all my concerns. I delivered the lecture with my usual enthusiasm and trained inflections and left the stage feeling nauseous. I went to the restroom and saw this pale face staring in the mirror, ready to vomit from the hypocrisy I forced my soul to commit.

Everything I had done and said as a faithful, believing Jehovah's Witness, I did with sincerity and complete conviction. Now I felt like a fraud and I couldn't and didn't want to continue living my life in this manner.

The second disturbing incident I want to share took place in autumn of 1997 when my 17-year-old daughter Sabrina told one of my statements to the elders of our

64

congregation. It was the comment: *"I have arrived at the conclusion that "the truth" is not the truth."* While I was attending a routine meeting of our body of elders, I was confronted unexpectedly with my statement. The purpose of the meeting was to prove that I was a "secret apostate" endangering the congregation. Men with whom I had friendly relationships for years were willing to "execute" me on the spot. I do not want to exaggerate, but the picture of a medieval witch hunt came to mind. They felt they had to take steps against me out of loyalty to God and to His organization. Thanks to my training in rhetoric and knowledge of all the internal rules and regulations, I was able to defend myself well and left them unable to take further action against me. Arriving home, I broke down in tears. My wife and my daughter observed me without any comment or word of consolation. People who were betrayed by their own family under the government of Hitler or in Communist systems, I imagine, must have had similar feelings.

The final step of the development was the end of my marriage. I do not want to write details about it or give the impression that I just want to blame my wife Gabriele, but what I will say about the matter is that the foundation of our marriage was our common faith as Jehovah's Witnesses. Our marriage ended after more than twenty years because I was not willing to stay in the same religion as my wife. We separated with a common understanding, as we did not see a chance to continue our marriage with me leaving this religion. Later there were rumors that I left my family because of another woman and that I was guilty of committing adultery. This is just not true, but there was no sense in fighting the rumor. It was easier for people to accept that I was immoral than to acknowledge the fact that I had found evidence against "the truth." It is not my intention to reveal private details of my former marriage. I can only say that I had a clean conscience and felt free before God with the agreement to separate and divorce.

There were not many that made efforts to talk to me or *to save* me. Probably many did not want to know what I really knew and thought, thus afraid to get into a conflict of conscience themselves.

Through my estranged wife, my father-in-law Hans

Krüger offered to help me spiritually. He wanted to arrange a meeting where his brother Helmut Krüger would be present. Being the "City Overseer", his brother had a position on the highest level of hierarchy in the city of Berlin. To my wife I commented: "I think they are the ones who need help, not me." Of course, this sounded insulting to two Jehovah's Witnesses who were convinced to have "the truth." I knew this could easily mean my excommunication as an apostate. Having two people against me present with no other witnesses, I agreed to the meeting under the condition that the conversation would be taped and that I could determine the topics to be discussed. This was rejected and since then I have never heard from my former father-in-law again. Indeed, neither he nor his brother expressed a desire to see me again. In the meantime both have passed away. Despite all of the good relationships I had during all those years, not one person ever tried *to save my soul*. Most likely because they were afraid of what I had to say.

In January of 1998 I attended the special seminar for elders together with hundreds of other men, but God's Spirit did not show me that I was on the wrong path. On the contrary, everything that I had read, heard and experienced confirmed my decision to separate from this religion and enter new spiritual ways with an open mind and heart. At the end of the second day of the seminar I submitted a letter addressed to the elders of my congregation in which I briefly explained why I would step down from all my "privileges" and responsibilities in the organization of Jehovah's Witnesses. Since then, I have never attended a service by Jehovah's Witnesses in a Kingdom Hall again.

Following this resignation, Jehovah's Witnesses were literally spying on my private life trying to find "evidence" of immorality. I was not going to allow an unjust excommunication on the grounds of apostasy, nor did I want others to have the impression that I left the religion because I was living an "immoral" life. This was the reason for my official declaration that I no longer want to be a member of Jehovah's Witnesses. As it is standard procedure this was publicly announced in the Kingdom Hall I had normally attended.

Since then, I have the same status as that of a *disfellowshipped* person. After this, not one of my former friends seeing me by coincidence in passing, would say hello or talk to me for fear of becoming excommunicated themselves.

Saddened and disturbed by my spiritual development, my brother Frank, with whom I had a very close relationship, stopped communication. Since I left the religion, I saw him only four times, at the funerals of my father and our grandmother, once picking up my mother from his house and at the funeral of my mother in December of 2014. In situations of family emergency, Jehovah's Witnesses are permitted to talk about necessary things with their excommunicated family members.

If the organization does not change the rules or if he is not willing to take the freedom and risk to ignore them, I will see my brother never again in my life. This is a very painful thought. Probably it hurts him too and he thinks that this is all my fault and that he would be glad to welcome me if I return to the organization.

People whom I have known since childhood, people whom I had tried to help spiritually, emotionally and materially outright ignore my greeting. People, for whom I was available for day and night, pass me by without a word or even a glance of acknowledgement and dismiss me as a complete stranger.

Why do they do that? They are not heartless or cold people without any feelings. They do it out of loyalty to God and to "His organization." Religious thinking is compromising their lives even in the smallest of details. I am trying to clearly demonstrate the kind of "monopoly" of minds and hearts by such a religion. It is so penetrating that one could negate any human feeling in an instant for the sake of remaining faithful to God's true organization as they know it.

Notably, my parents and both of my sisters Madelein and Esther have maintained a good relationship with me despite all these rules. My parents received and tolerated visits of elders "testing out" their loyalty and my "apostate" influence on them. But up to this time no steps have ever been taken against my family members. However, when my father died in October of 2004, no Christian love or compassion was shown to my mother from her congregation. She has been more or less socially abandoned with all her needs.

After my mother passed away in November of 2014 only "unbelievers" (non-Jehovah's Witnesses) have shared their compassion and feelings with me.

My daughter Sabrina had to experience very unpleasant judicial committee hearings, resulting in her being excommunicated. She has been psychologically and physically ill. She has accepted professional help and continues to recover little by little. Now at the age of 38, she still struggles to create a new life for herself.

Chapter 7

Feelings of being a victim
and having accumulated guilt myself

It is not easy for me to write this chapter, but it is very important for two reasons. First, because it must be demonstrated that under religious influence, a victim can become a person guilty of harming others. Secondly, I want to remain honest in relating my story and I do not write this book for personal justification or to accuse others for all the damage done. I am not only a victim but in turn blameworthy myself of doing harm. It is true I was influenced, but nobody forced me to become a Jehovah's Witness. This is why I also have to acknowledge my own guilt and admit it openly.

Of course, I feel victimized by a damaging religious influence. My thinking and my life had been dictated and manipulated by a religion that claims to be God's only organization on earth. This was possible because I was willing to believe it. Being convinced to be "in the truth"

72

and presumptuous enough to know what God's will was, I also became guilty of causing damage to others. Yes, others became victims because of me. I can no longer compensate for most of the damage I have done. It is very difficult for me to write about it, as I am embarrassed about things I thought, said and did. It is still saddening and very hurtful for me to think about some of the consequences of my actions.

The death of my son Manuel

This is probably the most difficult part of my confession. When my son Manuel was six years old, he became ill. He suffered from a T-cell Non-Hodgkin-Lymphoma. This is a systemic cancer which can affect the whole body, brain and bone marrow. Initially he underwent chemotherapy and radiation treatment to the head. For half a year he received this treatment while in the pediatric cancer station of the university clinic Rudolf Virchow in Berlin, with either his mother or myself always by his side. After this treatment he continued to receive chemotherapy for one and half more years as an outpatient. When he was eight years old he suffered a relapse, and died in our home six weeks later. Qualified personnel from the pediatric cancer clinic were available for him and us throughout the duration of his illness.

At this time small children with Non-Hodgkin-Lymphoma had a 75 % chance of survival. My son's chance of survival was less, as he did not respond well to the beginning of the therapy. As Jehovah's Witnesses we refused the transfusion of so called "principle blood components." This is why he did not receive the full dosage of cytostatic drugs (substances used in chemotherapy). One side effect of the medication is that thrombocytes (platelets) drop to a life threatening level. As we refused the transfusion of thrombocytes, the dosage of medication and the amount of radiations had to be lowered as well.

When a relapse occurs, a bone marrow or stem cell transplantation is usually considered. While Jehovah's Witness do allow bone marrow transplantations, this procedure was out of the question, as the church would not agree to the transfusion of erythrocytes (red blood cells used for the transportation of oxygen). After bone marrow or stem cell transplantation the body cannot produce its own blood for a certain period of time (at that time about ten days). This is why a transfusion of erythrocytes becomes necessary. But taking erythrocytes is not permitted by Jehovah's Witnesses. Hence, there is a contradiction, one against all logical reasoning because the bone marrow is practically "the factory" of blood. Produced stem cells in the bone marrow are much more similar in consistency to full blood cells than erythrocytes which appear everywhere in the body, like, for example, in urine.

Nobody knows whether our son Manuel would have survived taking full advantage of all the medical options. Shamefully I have to admit that as parents it was more important to make sure that our son would not receive a transfusion of principle blood particles than it was to accept all possible medical treatment for a full 75 % chance victory over cancer. I carry this thought and guiltiness in my heart always. I believed that obeying a divine law as interpreted by "His organization" was more important than optimal treatment of my little son. I was convinced that we would get him back in the resurrection and that no permanent damage could be done by his death. I loved my son with the whole heart of a father and I would have done anything for his happiness, except violate this "divine law" interpreted by men.

My tears falling as I write this cannot even fully express what I am feeling.

Psychological damage done to my daughter Sabrina

I have always loved my daughter Sabrina very much and tried to show this by being a good father since she was born in 1980. But it was very important for me to educate her according to Bible principles as they were explained to us by "God's organization." Sadly, she suffered psychological damage, but perhaps she will be ready sometime in the future to talk and write about her own experiences. I know her insights would be of benefit to others recovering from the psychological damage done by religion.

These are some of the things I came to regret and now pass them on:

I regret most of all that I shielded my daughter from reality by living in a seemingly "perfect world" where I trusted the people in this religion too much. In a certain way I was "blinded", and did not prevent things that happened within this "perfect world" which caused her grave damage.

I repent every act of "physical discipline" which both of my children received. It was always painful for me, as beating children is completely against my nature. But I believed that God wanted parents to discipline their children physically by teaching them obedience and respect for divine laws (Proverbs 13:24). It did not happen often, but I am guilty of having beaten my children. Today, Jehovah's Witnesses do not encourage anymore the beating of children. This would bring about legal conflicts with the law of many countries. But it is not easy to interpret Scriptures in the Bible about physical punishment of children symbolically.

I regret the existence of an unnecessary list of rules which my children had to obey.

I regret that my small children had to attend one one-hour and two two-hour church services per week while sitting quietly, although they did not understand anything. (Jehovah's Witnesses do not have provision for child care during their church services. Children have to get dressed up. When they do not sit quietly, they are taken out and return after having been disciplined.)

I regret I had taught them that only we have the truth and that all other people who do not change will be judged and executed by God.

I regret countless hours spent in our congregation's activities and in our evangelizing work instead of giving this time to my children.

My daughter had to go through so many hard experiences:

Experiencing the death of her brother. What a nightmare for a ten year old girl!

I am sorry that because of my leaving this religion our daughter had to experience separation and divorce of her parents and that she had to go through many difficult experiences herself. Her "perfect world" had been destroyed; but I did not see any other alternative to my decision.

She was excommunicated by a "judicial committee", some of these men being immoral themselves in their thinking and acting. Being still a teenager she had to confess and respond to these men being on her own. No one was permitted to be at her side in those hearings, someone who could have supported her or witnessed the way they were treating her. It is these men who in reality deserve punishment! I am still full of anger when I think about the way she was treated. These are the names of the committee members responsible for the damage done:

Jürgen Kessler (chairman),
Siegfried John and Miguel Ruiz

In the past, I often felt helpless towards my daughter. If I could, I would take away the damage she has suffered. Now, I can just let her know that as a father I always loved her, but that religious influence had directed my love into wrong paths. This is one of my deepest regrets.

In the course of years my belief in the truthfulness of our

religion also became her personal conviction. In her teenager years she once approached me seeking help with some intimate problems bothering her conscience. But it was not possible for me to take away her guilt feelings, as my way of reasoning was contradicting the published rules of Jehovah's Witnesses. This is why she turned to other elders in the congregation to "confess her sins", causing further suffering for herself. I am not talking about any committed crime, but about normal worries and problems of a teenager but which were considered "sinful" by "God's organization."

Finally, when I left my religion she turned against me. Obedience and faithfulness towards the organization was now more important than a relationship with her father. Now she was even willing to present accusations against me, talking to the elders and cutting off any contact with me. It was clear she did not want any communication between us. I had no chance to explain to her the reasons for my changed insights. But was it not me who educated her in this intolerant faith?

I am grateful that I had opportunities to see Sabrina and visit with her frequently in past years. She enjoys a very good relationship to her little sister Amelie and to my second wife Patricia. This makes me very happy.

I condemned my parents and my sister

While I was a missionary, my sister Madelein fell in love with an excommunicated Jehovah's Witness while on vacation. My parents showed understanding for her feelings and were willing to help, doing everything they could to assist this young man in getting reinstated into the religion.

Due to the kindness my parents exhibited, heavy organizational pressure was placed on them, especially my father. After several meetings with elders of his congregation Berlin Lichtenrade, letters to the Branch Office and a hearing with a so called "committee of appeal", the Branch Office of Jehovah's Witnesses in Germany decided to remove my father from all his privileges in the congregation. He was considered almost "a rebel" because he compared his feelings towards his excommunicated future son-in-law with the feelings of the father in Jesus' parable of the lost son. His lifelong faithful service in the congregations of Jehovah's Witnesses did

84

not count. Remaining faithful to man-made "rules" was considered more important than his merciful attitude towards this young man. He became ill emotionally, had a nervous breakdown and went into early retirement. Despite of this, he continued to attend religious meetings and remained a faithful Jehovah's Witness until his death, even sending money donations to the Watchtower Society. After he died, no mention or honor was given to his lifelong activities with Jehovah's Witnesses.

Being loyal to "God's Organization" during this time in my life, I took an opposing stand against my parents and sister. Naturally, today I am regretful and ashamed of the things I stated and wrote in letters. Faithfully obeying rules of a religious organization was more important to me than human relationships and feelings.

Luckily my parents and my sister Madelein did not bear a grudge against me. After being reinstated, this young man and my sister were married and I was even asked to perform the wedding ceremony. Similarly, when I left this religion they showed much more tolerance and love towards me in comparison to how they were treated by myself years before.

My participation in "judicial committees"

Jehovah's Witnesses are told to confess to an "elder" of their congregation certain "sins", of which there are lists and exact instructions and definitions. This "elder" communicates the information to the entire body of elders and then a "judicial committee", consisting of at least three men is appointed to meet with the "sinner." In this meeting with the judicial committee, a decision will be made whether the "sinner" will get excommunicated or will receive a private or public chastisement. Even if the person does not get excommunicated, restrictions and removal of privileges will be imposed. Crimes like murder, sexual violation, child abuse or theft would not be reported to the police. (The procedures of handling crimes have been modified since there were scandals revealing child abuse in the Catholic Church and court cases drew public attention to the issue.) I mention those things because they really happen although most Jehovah's Witnesses don't know about it because such matters are kept confidential. Congregation Elders claim to have the same right as that of a priest in remaining confidential. This is done in order to avoid publicity and not to "disgrace God's name or His organization."

The men of such judicial committees are usually not equipped to deal with psychological problems in a professional and mature way, child abuse and addictions of all kinds require a trained professional. Enormous damage is done to Jehovah's Witnesses in this regard. Women and girls have to present their intimate lives in front of three or more men who may have their own sexual problems. They depend on their mercy and do not have the right of a legal assistant or the presence of another person who has their confidence and could testify in their behalf in such situations. If they get excommunicated they lose their families, friends and all social contacts.

I have to confess being guilty of having participated as a member of such judicial committees and hearings. I had always tried to show compassion and tactfulness by never agreeing to an excommunication unless persons involved wished it so. Unfortunately, being a part of this "judicial system", I was not able to prevent a tremendous amount of emotional suffering and likewise, unable to avoid taking judgmental positions in moral issues. I regret this very much.

Shortly before I left the organization I refused to participate in a judicial committee. Due to the stand I took on a situation under review, I, myself, was put under suspicion. In this case we received instructions from the German Branch Office of the Watchtower Society to excommunicate a woman even before the hearing began and I just did not agree. My conscience did not permit me to feel guilty in this situation.

A woman had been beaten and violated over a long period of time by her husband who was also a Jehovah's Witness. With help of her doctor she was able to receive therapy in a clinic. There she found a certain emotional stability by talking to an older gentleman who showed her some compassion for her problems. He gave her his address and telephone number in the event of a future emergency situation. After returning home and being abused again by her husband, the woman fled finding refuge in the home of this old man in Berlin. She got in touch with our congregation and asked me for help. I wrote a letter to the elders of the congregation concerning her husband, informing them about the crime which that man had committed against his wife. He denied everything and claimed that his wife had left him without just cause, for another man. Our sister had taken refuge in the big apartment of this old man, showing her gratitude by keeping up his household. As she shared an apartment with a man, we were asked to excommunicate her because of adultery. Her husband, however, continued as an accepted member of his congregation.

In missionary homes of Jehovah's Witnesses male and female missionaries, not married to each other, sometimes spent days and nights together being alone in the same apartment. I know this from my own experience. Nobody seemed to worry about this then.

I regret that I was an active member of such a system of injustices, causing unimaginable damage to people.

90

Being a chairman of a "hospital liaison committee"

By reason of falsely interpreted Bible scriptures, Jehovah's Witnesses refuse the transfusion of the following blood components: erythrocytes, leucocytes, thrombocytes and plasma. However, it is permitted to receive fractions of those blood particles, i.e. coagulation factors and albumin. Also permitted are stem cell, bone marrow and organ transplantations. The use of certain surgical methods such as a "cell saver", which receives the blood and leads it back through closed systems in the body are also allowed. Nonetheless, all these many details and rules are always subject to change. Today something may be permitted while yesterday it could cause someone to be excommunicated.

Within the Witness Organization exists a worldwide hospital information service located in the headquarters in the USA and each of the Branch Offices in different lands. Additionally, there are hospital liaison committees that try to locate doctors sympathetic to the needs of Jehovah's

Witnesses patients and hospitals who were willing to respect the decisions of these medical professionals in regard to these patients. Members of these hospital liaison committees are called to give counsel, recommendations and information. They are also called upon to act as intermediaries between medical personnel, lawyers, judges and individual Jehovah's Witnesses.

However, people continue to have health complications or even die (according to an estimate 3 per day worldwide) because they decide in favor of the currently accepted knowledge and rules published by a few non-professionals who happen to be members of the Governing Body of Jehovah's Witnesses.

Gene Smalley, senior member of the writing staff in the headquarters of Jehovah's Witnesses once told me: "We are submitting problems and suggestions to the Governing Body for a solution or change of rules. Until the majority finally understands, agrees and is willing to vote for change, sometimes this could takes years."

In the meantime people suffer and die.

I was chairman of a hospital liaison committee and I accumulated much guilt in cooperating and supporting such a preposterous system. Regretfully, as a representative of this religious organization, I defended the official doctrines with all its regulations regarding blood transfusions. This affected the lives and well-being of many people.

People whom I convinced
to become Jehovah's Witnesses

Before one becomes a Jehovah's Witness, it is necessary to attend an instructive program for many months. The insider name for this is "Home Bible Study." Step by step the attendee is lead to make decisions and changes in his/her life until he or she can get finally baptized and become one of Jehovah's Witnesses. I have instructed many people and conducted a countless number of Home Bible Studies.

With what I had taught as a representative of my former religion, people have lost friends and families. Others were willing to give up their profession or end memberships or association with political parties, institutions, churches, sports teams, clubs and perhaps enjoyable hobbies. Books, pictures, religious or political paintings, items or jewelry have been thrown out. Ending observance of almost all holidays was recommended. People changed their outward appearance and their way of

94

thinking and speaking. Depending on the background of an individual, the list of changes one must carry out before becoming a Jehovah's Witness is indeed lengthy.

I am guilty of motivating people to make these lifestyle changes in their lives and they were certainly not according to God's will but to human interpretation.

Here is one of many typical examples I can share. While in my missionary assignment in Spain I was preaching in the house of a family with five children living in Zaragoza. The father Jose Valencia was a co-pilot in the Air Force. In two years he would have been retiring and going back into civil life. By virtue of our "Bible Study" he decided to leave the Air Force before fulfilling his contract. He lost all rights to his retirement, had to leave the house that belonged to the Air Force, and was faced with the problem of taking care of a big family.

Regretfully, I think back on these situations and how my missionary activity had such an influence on the lives of so many people.

My influence as a public speaker

After listening to my lectures and my counsel, people went home feeling strengthened in their faith and in their loyalty to our religious organization. I always talked positively and with enthusiasm about our organization and its doctrines. I tried to create and promote a spirit of joy, faith and loyalty. I never talked about my doubts and my internal knowledge of the organization. I did this having the best intentions and being personally convinced about "being in the truth." But this did not make the things that I have said and done right.

People should be warned and educated about the dangers of the influence of religious organizations. To my regret, I have encouraged people to follow a religion with obedience, humility and faith.

Chapter 8

Thoughts about future perspectives
for my former religion

It is my opinion that unless revolutionary changes occur in the present structure, the end or the complete insignificance and almost disappearance of the religious organization to which I belonged will come to pass within the foreseeable future although the number of Jehovah's Witnesses seems to increase. Here are some thoughts and conclusions regarding this idea.

A first thought:

Jehovah's Witnesses discourage *"worldly education"* and due to this there are very few with an academic degree. There are also very few open-minded thinkers as sooner or later they are classified as "dangerous apostates." Without open-minded thinkers who are willing to go "new ways" no real spiritual development is possible. If there are no drastic changes in the attitude about academic education, soon there will be neither an intellectual base nor capable leadership left.

A second thought:

With the complicated doctrinal explanations in connection with the year 1914 they have really marked their own deadline. How long can they maintain explanations that the year 1914 marked the beginning of the "last days" and beginning of "Christ's invisible presence as king in heaven"? The appointment of an "earthly channel of God to distribute spiritual food at its appropriate time" has been connected with the year 1914. (Matthew 24:45-47) If the teaching about 1914 is dropped, there has to be a new explanation about God's time and way of appointing an "earthly channel."

The Watchtower magazine indicated shortly before the year 2000, that the "last days" when Noah lived before the huge deluge lasted 120 years (Matthew 24:37 "For just as the days of Noah were, so the presence of the Son of man will be.") This now gives them a "breathing space" till the

98

year 2034, then what? Maybe there is hope those new generations will not remember former statements or will not do research in "old" publications.

A third thought:

According to the official doctrine of Jehovah's Witnesses, which has not been revised completely yet, the last "anointed" had been selected by Christ in the mid 1930's. The number of 144,000 co-kings with Christ, mentioned in the Book of Revelation 7:4 and 14:1, was complete in 1935. After this year there were only "substitute appointments" as a replacement for unfaithful Christians.

In The Watchtower of May 1, 2007 this explanation has been modified in one sentence, saying that God has chosen to select some "anointed" after 1935. This clarification had to come! All present eight members of the "Governing Body" have been born or baptized after 1935! Presently 19,521 Jehovah's Witnesses confess to be "anointed" with an increase in numbers yearly. In 2005 8,524 claimed to be "anointed." Most of them have been born and baptized after 1935.

In the "Governing Body" of the Witnesses and in the responsible writing staff of their publications, there are no "anointed" who could have possibly received their call at the time of their baptism before 1935. The leadership of this organization is made up exclusively by "substitute anointed" (receiving the call after 1935) or by men who do not even claim to have this "anointed status." In general, this is not known by Jehovah's Witnesses and it is not easily recognizable either, as there is no published record with names, birthdays, baptism dates or claims to belong to the "anointed."

The Watchtower of July 15, 2013 has published for the first time in history eight names of the members of the "Governing Body" and their pictures, one of them passed away in the meantime. He has been replaced.

How long will they be able to keep this reality a secret? What kind of explanations will they find so followers continue believing in the progressive revelation of God's truth through his earthly channel? The passing of time since 1914 and the fact that the end of the world has not come will make it difficult to explain things. Only a radical "new light of truth" could help. But what will that be and how many will believe and accept it?

In the meantime another new and absurd definition of "the generation which will not pass away" has been given which gives them time till half of this century has passed.

Dear Jehovah's Witnesses: For how much longer will you accept patiently and humbly new explanations and permit getting fooled that way?

There are rumors that there will be a name change: Christian Congregation of Jehovah Worshipers (JW).
I don't know how reliable this information is.

There seems to be a tendency to give less importance to their house-to-house preaching activity. More people are reached through the Internet or at special newsstands in downtown areas. Who knows, maybe they will slow down or cease the unproductive house-to-house activity one day. Much less distributing of printed literature is done because of the availability of publications on their website jw.org. All this could lead to a change or stop of having to turn in a monthly report about one's preaching activity. In January 2016 there has been already a change using now a simplified report slip. What a relief this would mean for the individual Witness!

It is not impossible that there will come about a change in the "blood issue": They may continue to stick faithfully to their Bible interpretation of not taking blood, but tolerate the acceptance of blood components, which in reality are not blood anymore. This would mean a solution for all medical emergencies as nowadays blood components are transfused as a standard treatment, depending on the individual health condition and necessity.

Maybe they will loosen up in their treatment of excommunicated members. Now it is tolerated again to applaud when the announcement of a reinstatement of a disfellowshipped member is made.

Maybe they will become even a little bit more tolerant toward birthdays. Remembering birthdays once was acceptable in the early days of the organization.

All of this would result in less criticism and controversy from the public and less "apostates" would be the result.

Knowing so many precious people in this organization, I would be happy if this religion would become a more tolerant home for Jehovah's Witnesses. However I do not have any hopes that they will give up their fundamentalist thinking and organizational structures.

Chapter 9

Conclusions and a personal outlook

While enjoying an evening at theater in Berlin where my wife Patricia was performing in the musical "The Huntchback of Notre Dame", during intermission an "elder" of my former religion recognized me. Having the courage to approach me, he told me that many would be happy if I would return to the organization. I expressed my appreciation for the fact that he approached me and for his words, which showed his sympathy for me. I explained that coming back would be a "step backwards" in my life since in the meantime, I have been able to prove biblically that "the truth" is not true. He answered "You may know more than I do, but I know it for sure, I feel it in my heart that we do have the truth." Well, I know this feeling, but it is false and it does not stand up to close examination. One has to pay a high price in life for this feeling and I am not willing to pay it any longer.

For their religious well-being, many people need the
104

feeling of belonging to a community. Even if they do not agree with everything; belonging to a church or a religion gives them a feeling of security, support and significance in life. People's needs vary; for some, much freedom and an environment of tolerance is necessary. For others, an orthodox or even fundamentalist worldview is important to achieve stability in life. Some desire clear and strict guidelines for their lives and want to clearly define good and bad as black and white. Others, confronted with authoritarian structures, lack the possibilities to contradict and questions.

Is it beneficial to belong to a church or is it better to keep away from institutionalized religion? The famous German writer Hermann Hesse made the following observation:

"For the majority of people it is very good to belong to a church or to a faith. The one who separates from it, walks first of all on a road of loneliness, even longing again for the former community. Only at the end of his road will he discover that he has entered a new large but invisible community embracing all people and religions. He will get poorer concerning everything dogmatic and national, but will get richer by means of belonging to a brotherhood of spirits of all times and all nations and languages."

At this point in my life I do not have any desire to belong to a church or religion. I do not know of any solid reasoning that could motivate me to follow a specific faith or belong to any religion to secure my salvation or maintain peace in my soul.

My spiritual, emotional and physical well-being has become a touchstone for my thoughts and actions. I respect the value of each human being, either as individuals or organized in groups; as long as they do not harm others, but respect the life and dignity of their fellow men, women and children. It is not my right to look condescendingly on people just because they do not share my opinion or viewpoint. Every human being is in a different stage of spiritual development and very frequently, over a long period of time, we do not recognize how false and harmful we may have been thinking and acting.

I am grateful for people who have been tolerant, forgiving and patient with me despite all the mistakes I made in my past. Although having had the best of intentions, my thinking was narrow-minded for many decades and I have harmed people because of it. Having had my life consistently determined for me, I was just not able to see things clearly. I was just not able to see things from a different point of view. My mind was closed to evidence and logic reasoning because of being convinced and living self-confidently with the right and wrong of an "artificial world of truth."

I was part of a *closed, inorganic world* in the midst of the real world. In *"The New World Society"* (the name Jehovah's Witnesses give to themselves) it seems that logical answers are given to all of life's fundamental questions. For example, happiness is promised when you obey all biblical principles as they are understood by the organization. Witnesses claim that their current understanding of the Bible is "the truth." But as I have said, this claim does not withstand close examination.

Additionally, they call themselves "God's sons of freedom"; although living as a Jehovah's Witness means to give up freedom of thought along with many personal choices. In reality, Jehovah's Witnesses are victims of fundamentalist brain washing that is fueled by a constant threat of fear. A fear which keeps people inside this religion. It is the warning that thinking and acting differently than the organization's explained will of God, results in the loss of God's blessings, loss of happiness and loss of the prospect of everlasting life in an earthly paradise. The fact that I was able to liberate myself from this "world" and that kind of thinking, almost appears miraculous to me.

There is no reason to fear that there is no other spiritual alternative. There is also no reason to fear loneliness because of losing family and friends. As I have found, there are many social, spiritual and religious options. There are many worthy, sincere and nice people in this world who are willing to love and appreciate you without giving importance to whether you are a member of a religion or not.

While I was struggling and transforming myself spiritually, I prayed intensely for God's guidance, wisdom and even His discipline and correction for more than a year. If I really was a member of the "true" religion, why did He not correct me, why did He not help me to understand my doubts and questions differently? Did He not want to answer my prayers? Had I not been worthy? What did I do to lose His guidance and blessings in my life? Or could '*the truth*' be that He gave me the strength to liberate myself from religious oppression?

Who am I to give an answer to these questions? I just know one thing for sure: I am enjoying peace of mind and heart. Despite the drastic changes in my thinking and life, I did not really lose anything valuable. In all aspects of life, compared to what I lost, I have received much more in return. Of course, I lost a lot time in my life and spent many years with senseless activities. If it is true that life is a school of learning, it took me many years to learn certain lessons. But it is not the number of years of life that are important for our happiness; it is the quality of life that counts. In one of my "spiritual writing projects" I am gathering my conclusions about this subject under the topic: "Quality of life: What factors contribute to it and what things diminish or destroy it?" I suppose constant reflection is one of the "side effects" of the experience I have shared with you.

Why it has taken me so long to chronicle my life and write my conclusions, I do not know. Perhaps my concern about the feelings of my parents and siblings, or maybe I was looking for a way to write without "throwing dirt" on my former friends. Probably it was also important for me to gain a certain distance and investigate walking on new spiritual paths instead of spending all my time and energy thinking and talking about my past.

The day before I gave the aforementioned lecture, feeling like a hypocrite as I did, happened to be my 45th birthday. Before the talk I had the opportunity to go for a walk in nature and I still remember how I raised my eyes to heaven and promised myself that the next 45 years will turn out to be the best ones in my life! More than twenty-one years after this I still feel the energy and truth of that promise. My 50th birthday year was an unbelievable climax in my life and now being in my 67th year I am experiencing the best phase in my life so far. It is getting better and I feel I have really experienced the truthfulness of the following words of Henry Thoreau:

"I have learned this at least by my experiment: that if one advances confidently in the direction of his dreams, and endeavors to live the life which he has imagined, he will meet with a success unexpected in common hours."

I am concluding with the desire that this book may help desperate people who are imprisoned in their way of thinking and living by religious or political ideologies and organizations. I wish them courage, energy and above all faith in themselves to liberate theirs souls and be able to live in harmony with their authentic self.

EPILOGUE

Many would like to know what I believe and think now. I have been very hesitant answering these questions because people respond very sensitively about questions of faith. Questioning their beliefs is like shaking the fundaments of their lives. Many can't tolerate being confronted with doubts about the beliefs that have given significance and stability in their lives. It is likened to the fear of being pushed down into an abyss. There is this enormous panic that one's world view could be destroyed and there is no alternative.

My own experience is that I was able to doubt my world view. I was able to reject it and I did not lose my stability by not having an alternative world view available. I lost the pressure of having to believe in something and I did not become hopeless because of it. I did not lose my peace of heart and mind, and I did not lose my positive outlook on life.

I am being asked questions based on three topics:

Is The Bible God's inspired Word?

Is the Christian faith the only acceptable way to God?

Does God exist?

Here are some of my thoughts.

Is The Bible God's inspired Word?

According to most Christian religions 66 books of the Old Testament and the New Testament from Genesis to Revelation belong to The Bible.

It is a fact that there is no claim anywhere in The Bible that all 66 books have been written under God's inspiration. Yes, there are some Scriptures which talk about an inspiration of God, but this never applies to all 66 books. These texts refer to individual prophets and parts of the Old Testament. In the New Testament only the book Revelation (Apocalypses) claims to be passed on directly from God.

A claim in itself is not proof; but let's keep this in mind. The Bible itself does not claim that all 66 books in their entirety were written under God's inspiration. There is a variety of claims by Christian religions. Some believe that every word of the entire Bible was inspired by God. Others say that the writing of The Bible was supervised and controlled by God's Spirit. In addition, many Christians believe that The Bible is God's Word because it contains words from Jesus Christ, from Christian writers and from prophets who were all blessed and guided by God.

It is interesting to know some historic facts about the canon of The Bible and how it came into existence. People who believe that the current collect of 66 books make up The Bible, also have to believe that God used popes and bishops of the Catholic Church to decide this. In the 4th century or later, these popes and bishops determined what belonged to The Bible and what did not. It was only a long time after the 1st century when decisions were made as to which of the many existing gospels, books of apocalypses and letters of apostles would be accepted as part of the Bible canon and considered as "God's Word."

The following "evidences" for divine inspiration of The Bible are mentioned frequently:

Fulfillment of Bible prophecies.

Historic and scientific accuracy.

Wisdoms contained in the Scriptures.

Old age and wide distribution of The Bible.

All the above characteristics also apply to other writings, books of ancient times and modern history.

Bible prophecies contain information frequently kept in very general terms offering a wide range of interpretation. Some seem to be detailed and specific but their time of writing cannot be determined without doubts as to its chronological authenticity.

Many historic documents exist that are accurate and reliable, proving that people of the antiquity had amazing scientific knowledge.

It is true that Bible Scriptures contain wise sayings. But there are also many books which can compete with The Bible in this regard. I found more statements of wisdom in a variety of unrelated books, than I have found in The Bible.

There are writings older than The Bible, and books with a wide distribution more popular than The Bible in certain parts of the world.

The Bible continues to be a historically interesting collection of books. It has given faith, a purpose in life and a moral guideline for many people. But it remains a personal religious opinion to see The Bible as God's Word, maybe even his only Word to mankind. This claim is not supported by The Bible itself or by scientific evidences.

Is the Christian faith the only acceptable way to God?

The history and dispersion of the Christian faith demonstrates two of these aspects:
Christian believers found personal fulfillment, happiness and moral standards in their lives.
Unbelievable sufferings and bloodshed are historic facts of Christianity.

In religious organizations naming Jesus Christ as their savior, you find both:
People with strong faith, moral principles, deeds of love *and* grave emotional and physical suffering.

The issue for me is the Christian claim of exclusiveness. I can easily accept it when a Christian says that his faith is the best way *for him* to get closer to God and live a happy life. But in claiming this religious superiority, one learns that the one and only way to God is believing in Jesus Christ and accepting him as your savior. It is truly believed that this is *the only way* to obtain forgiveness of sins and salvation.

Another issue is the forgiveness of sins. I cannot understand why and in what way a new born child is a sinner. Of course, I may make mistakes in my life or I may get sick, but I still cannot see why this makes me a sinner. I cannot understand that my daughter will not be saved just because she was never baptized as a baby or because she has "unbelieving" parents.

An additional concern occupying my mind is what the Bible teaches. Adam the perfect human being, brought sin and death into the world because of disobeying the law of God. The perfect human Jesus sacrificed his human life to liberate us from sin and death. Why does the Christian God limit his divine power because of this self-imposed rule? According to the Koran, Allah feels able to forgive without sacrifices and ransom. If the perfect human life of God's son Jesus Christ was the required ransom price, why did he have to die in such a cruel way? A perfect human life was required but not torture and a painful death!

People of all religions claim that God is listening and answering their prayers. We read and hear about "miracles" in Christian and non-Christian religions. Are they all right, or are members of just one religion right? Perhaps they are all mistaken?

I have become spiritually more awake in recent years and I am excited when I think about my future life. Although my beliefs about The Bible, the Christian faith and religion have changed, I am enjoying peace of heart and mind. There is a tolerance and spiritual awakening in my life as never before.

Does God exist?

I can't answer this question clearly and definitely. An answer may also depend on how one defines "God" or how one imagines him or her. Is God an energy, a part of us, something in our subconscious, something abstract which you cannot define? Or is He an invisible being with a personality existing outside the material universe?

Before I give attention to the question directly, I would like to say the following. I am in the position to compare two different time spans in my life. Apart from the first five years of my life, forty years had been molded under the influence of the God whom I worshiped and the religion I practiced. I prayed regularly and intensely. I believed to see His answers to my prayers and to feel His spirit in my life; and I was willing to structure my entire life under His guidance. There was almost nothing that I planned in my life without seeking His guidance. I admit, I was basically happy during those years.

In comparison, no thought about God or religion has influenced my life during the past twenty-one years. I lived so to speak "godless" or "nondenominational." These last twenty-one years have been in reality by far the best time in my life thus far. I feel spiritually, physically and emotionally better than ever before. My life quality has been incomparably better. Whether God does exist or not, I would always decide for the kind of life I have had during the last twenty-one years. I am looking forward to my future and I am enjoying right now the second year of my retirement. I feel relaxed when I think about old age and death as the end of life. I have come to the conclusion that there is probably no God when I consider the decades "with and without God" in my life. For the way I want to live and for my happiness, it is not important anymore whether God exists or not.

The key question certainly is: Did the universe and life come into existence by the creative act of an intelligent being, whom we call God or Creator?

The answer is: No one can answer this with one hundred percent certainty. Our knowledge does not permit us to come to a final conclusion. Irrefutable scientific evidence does not exist to fully support one or the other opinion. There are logical sounding reasons and numerous facts presented by both sides. In the end, one has to accept and believe what one has chosen as their personal truth and what seems most probable to the individuals thought process.

Of course, this does not mean that the weight of evidence in favor or against the existence of God is balanced equally. No, the existing evidence leads to conclude that the existence of God is not very likely. But it is not easy for the average educated person to really understand and examine existing scientific evidence and reasoning. Unless one has done intensive university studies in biology, physics, chemistry, geology, archeology, paleontology, genetics, astronomy, history or another subject related to religion and God, one is only able to obtain a rather superficial knowledge. For those able to obtain this knowledge, scientific evidence against the existence of God sounds very convincing.

However, apart from scientific knowledge, the existence of God would leave us with many questions. Some of these questions I am asking in my book *Questions for God* (available through Amazon or bookstores). Questions help us see the essential part of things. Not only are they an important tool in helping to recognize problems, or possible solutions, but they are a great help in obtaining knowledge.

But no one can claim with any certainty to possess the complete truth. We have all reason to keep an open mind and maintain a tolerant attitude while examining or considering different viewpoints.

THE TRUTH, *that is* true

The worldwide community of spiritual, tolerant and peaceful people is increasing in number. More people than ever contribute to a world worth living in. More and more people are less interested in any ideology, specific religion or faith that claims to possess the *only* truth. They refuse to be patronized by doctrines and rules of institutionalized religion. These are people who are not willing to allow others to control their conscience, freedom of choice or dictate details of their life. An attitude of tolerance is increasing even in orthodox religions with a tolerance to respect the dignity and conscience of the individual.

Many exciting spiritual ideas exist and new ones continue to evolve. All of them deserve tolerance and respect. All the different paths and forms of development in the search of a peaceful and better life on earth, have their legitimate place. Each concept deserves to be considered as a possible answer to the challenging issues of our day. Any explanation, idea and solution deserves acknowledgement, especially if it is presented in a non-dogmatic way.

I have found that the following principles work as a guideline for my life:

I watch how decisions, habits and life style affect my spiritual, emotional and physical well-being.

I make an effort not to say or do anything which could harm other people, other living beings or the environment of our planet earth.

I am always looking for opportunities to contribute to the well-being of others.

I do not want to be dogmatic or fanatic about anything ever again, but strive to keep an open mind to new ideas and factual evidence.

Recommendations for additional reading:

Crisis of Conscience, by Raymond Franz

In Search of Christian Freedom, by Raymond Franz

Jonathan Livingston Seagull, by Richard Bach

Siddhartha, by Hermann Hesse

The True Believer, by Eric Hoffer

The Canon, by Natalie Angier

50 Reasons People Give for Believing in a God,
by Guy P. Harrison

Questions for God, by Dieter Parczany

PART 2

INFORMATION

ABOUT JEHOVAH'S WITNESSES

Many who know my story or read my book want to know more about Jehovah's Witnesses and their beliefs. In the second part of this book I will present information and facts about Jehovah's Witnesses without additional commentaries.

Organizational structures, instructions, provisions, names, terms and also an understanding of doctrines or certain Scriptures of The Bible are constantly changing. They call this "new light" which God gives to his people at its "proper time." I made an effort to update the information available to me in January 2019.

Chapter 10

Early beginnings and history of Jehovah's Witnesses

There are three presidents of the Watchtower Bible & Tract Society in particular, who have influenced the history and beliefs of Jehovah's Witnesses: Charles Taze Russell, Joseph Franklin Rutherford and Nathan Homer Knorr in cooperation with his vice-president Frederick W. Franz.

Frederick W. Franz was the spiritual brain of the organization for approximately half a century. He had the final say when it came to questions of faith and doctrines. Besides some minor changes, up to this day his interpretations and explanations of The Bible are basically the fundament of the beliefs of Jehovah's Witnesses. He died in 1992.

He was the principal translator of the New World Translation, the Bible translation Jehovah's Witnesses use. His knowledge about the Hebrew and Greek language was self-taught. The anonymous Bible Translation Committee was not qualified for translating a Bible. Their names are known to insiders. At the end of 2013 a revised translation was published. Again the names of the members of the Translation Committee were not revealed.

After the death of Nathan Homer Knorr in 1977, the position of the president of the Watchtower Society lost its significance as far as the influence of organizational developments. Now the president serves only as a legal representative.

In previous decades, seven directors of the Watchtower Society served as the leading committee for the organization. Only in the year 1974 a "Governing Body" was established. Different committees made up of members of the "Governing Body" now were responsible for the oversight of the organization.

Raymond Franz, the nephew of Frederick Franz, was one of the "brains" behind this new arrangement. His influence and ideas became uncomfortable for some conservative members of the "Governing Body." In the beginning of the 1980's he was expelled from the "Governing Body" and a little later excommunicated. He wrote two remarkable books containing his story and included insider details which were never available before.

During the first six decades of the organization Jehovah's Witnesses were known as "Bible Students." Charles Taze Russell from Pennsylvania founded a Bible study group in the 1870's. At the age of 13 he separated from the Presbyterian religion of his parents and became a Congregationalist until the age of 18. Before developing his own ideas he sympathized for a while with beliefs of the Adventist Church. He became well known by publishing articles in newspapers and distributing tracts and books in front of churches before and after services. Soon The Watchtower was the principal magazine publishing ideas of this Bible Study Group.

According to the understanding of Jehovah's Witnesses, God blessed and guided this group of Bible Students. In the year 1919 it was said that God decided to select them

131

to be "His people." Jesus Christ, ruling as King in Heaven since 1914, appointed them to serve as His "faithful and discreet slave" in fulfillment of Matthew 24:45. According to the latest understanding, the expression "faithful and discreet slave" applies only to the "Governing Body" of Jehovah's Witnesses. From 1919 on Charles Taze Russell and his fellow believers were the only "true religion" or "God's people" in contrast to *all* other religions of the world. All other religions are part of the "World Empire of False Religion" or "Babylon the Great" (Revelation, chapter 18) and are condemned to eternal destruction.

Special characteristics during the time periods of the presidents of The Watchtower Society were:

Charles Taze Russell:
Developed and defended his Bible interpretations in publications and public discussions.
Expectation and announcement of the Second Coming of Christ in 1914.

Joseph Franklin Rutherford:

Expectation of "the end" in 1925. There were expectations and preparations of an earthly resurrection in California of some prophets of The Old Testament, which disappointingly did not occur.

Adopted the name "Jehovah's Witnesses" in 1931.

Nathan Homer Knorr:

Intensified international evangelizing activities by preaching from house to house.

Requests for each Witness to fill out a monthly or weekly report slip about his/her preaching activity.

Establishment of a "Theocratic Ministry School" (a training course in learning how to preach) for all members of the congregation.

The missionary school "Gilead" founded.

Introduction of "Home Bible Studies", which are courses to teach future Jehovah's Witnesses.

Prohibition of eating blood or accepting a blood transfusion.

Prohibition of celebrating religious holidays (Christmas, Easter, birthdays etc.)

Prohibition of the use of tobacco.

Prohibition of gambling.

Introduction of a judicial system where "judicial committees" are authorized to disfellowship (excommunicate).

Propagating that "the end" is near or at hand. A sense of urgency was created by announcing that 6,000 years of human history, since Adam's creation, would end in October 1975. People of this generation who were old enough to experience the events of 1914, would still be alive when "the end" came.

The 1970's saw a transition from the power of the president to the establishment of a "Governing Body." These were difficult years. Most of Jehovah's Witnesses do not know about the struggles that occurred in the headquarters in Brooklyn, New York at this time.

In January 2019 the "Governing Body" had eight members. The next level in the hierarchy of the organization are thirty-one men (January 2018) who are supporting the "Governing Body" as appointed "helpers" in different committees.

One can recognize three different religious organizations in their structure and doctrines when one compares the organization under the leadership of Russel, Rutherford and Knorr. If the rumor about a change of name (Jehovah Worshipers) is true, this could mean the beginning of a fourth renewal of the organization in structure and teaching.

Chapter 11

Organizational Structures

Jehovah's Witnesses claim to be part of a theocratic organization (directly guided and directed by God). But in reality, organizational structures show a system of hierarchy (see "Hierarchy Map" at the end of this chapter).

At the base of this hierarchy, are the *"publishers."* Those who qualify are permitted to participate in the evangelizing work in public. Each publisher is asked to turn in a monthly report slip containing information about hours spent, literature placed, return visits done and home Bible studies conducted. The report slip has been changed in January 2016 including also a report about the activities on the website jw.org. There are "regular publishers" (handing in reports for six consecutive months or more), "irregular publishers" (missing a month or more) and "inactive publishers" (not preaching for six months or more). They distinguish between "baptized and unbaptized publishers." All the information on the report

136

cards are kept on a file which is then examined by certain "elders."

About 10 to 150 "publishers" make up a *"congregation."*

Each congregation has a number of male *"ministerial servants."* They take care of technical assignments such as literature, finances, assigning territories to preach, and equipment in the Kingdom Hall etc. To be recommended as a "ministerial servant", males have to be baptized, at least 20 years old and meet certain other requirements. They are appointed during the visit of the "circuit overseer" who visits the congregation twice a year.

The *"elders"*, appointed by the circuit overseer in the name of the "Governing Body", are the ones who oversee and carry out the responsibilities in the local congregation. They lead in instructing, spiritual guidance, "judicial" decision making, etc. There is a "Coordinator", "Secretary" and "Service Overseer" (these three serve as the "service committee" of the congregation). In addition a "Watchtower Study Conductor" and a "Life and

Ministry Meeting Overseer" as well as "Group Overseers" are appointed.

A *"judicial committee"* consists of three or more "elders."
If one of the "elders" knows about a Witness committing
a sin, he informs the entire body of "elders." They decide
who and how many elders will make up the "judicial
committee" and which one of them will preside over the
case.

"Sins" that have to be treated by a "judicial committee"
include: premarital sex, petting between non married
partners, adultery, oral and anal sex practices,
homosexuality, abortions, attempts of suicide, use of
tobacco and drugs, drunkenness, gluttony, gambling, not
being politically neutral, participation in activities of
"false religion", eating or accepting the transfusion of
blood or principle blood components, lying, cheating,
slandering, spiritualistic practices, stealing, murder,
idolatry, child abuse, apostasy etc. The decisive factor for
excommunication is lack of repentance.

If one does not agree with the decision of the "judicial committee" one can appeal. He will be granted a hearing in front of a "committee of appeal" appointed by the "circuit overseer" and in the presence of the original "judicial committee." If both committees do not reach to an unanimous decision, the "service department" of the Branch Office makes a final decision.

Baptized men and women have the opportunity to be appointed as *"pioneers"* or *"fulltime ministers"* if they meet certain requirements.

"Auxiliary pioneers" are willing to preach 60 hours per month (requirement of hours is subject to change).

"Regular pioneers" promise to evangelize 90 hours per month or 1,000 hours per year (requirement of hours is subject to change). They are invited to attend a 10-day "pioneer school" course. Single "pioneers" also have the opportunity to attend a special school course.

Successful "pioneers" with good recommendations may be invited to become *"special pioneers."* They agree to preach 140 hours per month in any assigned territory of their country (requirement of hours is subject to change).

They receive a small allowance for living expenses from the Watchtower Society. Currently the arrangement of appointing "special pioneers" is in a process of being ended.

Twice a year 25 to 100 excellent "pioneers" are invited to become *"missionaries"* and attend the Watchtower Bible School of Gilead in New York. They agree to be assigned to any country and usually live with other "missionaries" in a "missionary home" where all expenses are covered. "Missionaries" and "special pioneers" get a few days of vacation each year, according to their age and years of service.

Fifteen to twenty congregations are united as a "circuit." Twice a year, they attend a two or one day assembly, usually held at an assembly hall built for this purpose. At these assemblies new Jehovah's Witnesses get baptized by total immersion in water. Beforehand, applicants for baptism must answer approximately one hundred questions to their local "elders." During this congress there is a "baptism talk" where afterwards those eligible for baptism must answer two more questions in public with the answer YES. One of the questions is a declaration that one has dedicated his/her life to Jehovah in the name of Jesus Christ. The other question confirms that the candidate recognizes becoming a member of God's only organization.

Each "circuit" has a *"circuit overseer"* appointed by the Branch Office in the name of the "Governing Body." He visits congregations twice a year for one week. The circuit overseer presents four talks in the local Kingdom Hall, participates in the evangelizing work with "publishers" and "pioneers", and holds special meetings with "pioneers", "ministerial servants" and "elders." He examines all congregation files, discusses problems, is responsible for appointing "ministerial servants" and "elders or overseers" and writes a report about his visit to the Branch Office.

Each year there is a regional assembly, and once in a while also an "international assembly" lasting between 3 and 7 days. Usually about 6,000 delegates are present at these assemblies, but there have been occasions with 150,000 or more people in attendance. "Circuit overseers" receive regular training at the Branch Office. "Elders" also receive special training every two or three years.

According to their website jw.org (2018) 8,579,909 active Jehovah's Witnesses are members of 119,954 congregations in 240 lands. They are supervised by the headquarters of Jehovah's Witnesses in Wallkill, New York and 87 Branch Offices worldwide. The headquarters and Branch Offices are called *"Bethel."*

Not long ago they stated that 20 billion pieces of printed material in 595 languages had been sent out during a period of ten years. No printing is reduced considerably as publications and information is made available online (jw.org).

They have farms which produce food for workers at "Bethel." The Watchtower Society sold their property in Brooklyn and moved their headquarters to Wallkill, Upstate New York.

"Bethelites" (workers at "Bethel" homes) are considered "full time ministers." They can be male or female. All "Bethelites" have a small room, get their meals in a dining hall and receive a small monthly allowance. They are members of a local congregation, but have additional meetings and training at "Bethel." Some are appointed as *"Bethel elders"* supervising different departments. Men in the "Service Department" handle the correspondence anonymously. This can be from congregations, circuits, answering questions, and offering solutions to problems. The Service Department is responsible for certain appointments and assignments.

Each Branch Office has a *"branch committee"* with three or more members, appointed by the "Governing Body." A permanent *"branch coordinator"* is appointed to serve as chairman, supervising all activities. All members of "branch committees" receive regular training under the supervision of the "Governing Body" in New York.

The "Governing Body" appoints special representatives, called *"headquarters representatives."* Once a year they visit Branch Offices and write a report to the "Governing Body" about the condition, problems and activities in each Branch Office and country.

Under the supervision of the "Writing Committee and Teaching Committee of the Governing Body" a writing staff writes anonymous books, articles in The Watchtower and Awake magazine, scripting weekly services for all congregations, outlining or scripting talks, assembly programs, and training seminars etc. Only certain questions and problems are chosen to be presented to the entire "Governing Body" to be determined by the majority. Most members of the "Governing Body" do not have an active share in writing publications.

In April 2015 for the first time names of thirty men have been published who have been appointed as *"helpers"* and who work as members of the different committees of the "Governing Body."

Resistance or contradiction to the men of a level above in the hierarchy is never tolerated and classified as rebellion against the theocratic order.

Ranking of Hierarchy

JEHOVAH
JESUS CHRIST

GOVERNING BODY

HELPERS OF THE GOVERNING BODY

HEADQUARTERS REPRESENTATIVES

BRANCH COMMITTEE COORDINATOR

BRANCH COMMITTEE

CIRCUIT OVERSEER

Hospital Liaison Committees●Construction Committees●
Assembly Committees●News Media Committees

BODY OF ELDERS OF A CONGREGATION
Coordinator●Secretary●Service Overseer●
Watchtower Study Conductor●Life and Ministry Meeting Overseer●
Group Overseers ● Judicial Committee

MINISTERIAL SERVANTS
Finances●Territory Assignment●Literature
Desk●Library●Maintenance●Usher● Hospital Visiting Group

PIONEERS *(men and women)*
Bethelites●Missionaries●Special Pioneers●Regular Pioneers●
Auxiliary Pioneers

PUBLISHERS *(men and women)*
Baptized
Non-Baptized

Chapter 12

Jehovah's Witnesses and money

As questions are frequently asked about how Jehovah's Witnesses are financed and who benefits from their money, I want to explain a few facts.

Jehovah's Witnesses use numerous registered corporations to finance and carry out their activities. Well known are The Watchtower Bible & Tract Society of New York, Inc. and The Watchtower Bible & Tract Society of Pennsylvania, Inc. There are no transparent reports about the total amount of income by voluntary contributions or any other means of income. Only very few people know the real figures. Moreover, the Watchtower Society and different corporations also own a large amount of real estate worldwide.

Nevertheless, there are no responsible men or individuals behind the scenes who enrich themselves personally or live a secret life of luxury. All responsible men live and work at the headquarters of Jehovah's Witnesses in Wallkill, New York or in one of their Branch Offices around the world. They live in a furnished one or two-bedroom apartment and do not pay rent or have any expenses. There are no costs for food and healthcare and all members at headquarters or Branch Offices receive a small monthly allowance. Outside there are "traveling representatives" who supervise activities of Jehovah's Witnesses in local congregations and at assemblies. There are also missionaries and so called "full time ministers", all of whom have their expenses paid by the Watchtower Society.

This should not be taken to mean that in their positions they do not have considerable financial benefits. Some are assigned to travel to inspect Branch Offices and to give lectures at assemblies and I can say with certainty some travel business class or first class while they are flying to their assignments. Moreover, traveling representatives of the Watchtower Society receive a great amount of financial assistance in the form of cash gifts from local Jehovah's Witnesses. Such non-taxable contributions enable them to purchase expensive clothing and technical equipment as well as going to restaurants and on vacations. As a result, many of them are living on a level that is unattainable for most families with low to medium income. In point of fact it is precisely because the largest part of their income is cash that their monthly "extra income" may be much higher than their taxable income.

Further, at various times and places in North America and Europe during the 1980's and 1990's printed literature began to be distributed free of charge. However, this was less because the Watchtower Society had suddenly become generous, than due to the fact that governments began claiming taxes for profits made on sold literature. As an example, I know that in the 1970's literature was sold for a price five times higher than the actual printing cost. Now, it is a much more lucrative enterprise to give literature away while at the same time accepting large tax-free donations unknown to the government. It is for this same reason that profitable food distribution at assemblies was stopped. The Watchtower Society is thus able to be financed by voluntary contributions while at the same time maintaining the status of a non-profit organization that does not have to pay taxes to the state.

In the end, it is precisely because it does not pay into any social security or retirement accounts that the organization of Jehovah's Witnesses offers no financial security for its representatives. In some countries, however, the courts have decided that Jehovah's Witnesses are required to pay a minimum amount to the social retirement system for former representatives who quit their activities and inquire of it. In other countries former fulltime Jehovah's Witnesses who leave their activities or the organization do not benefit from any social security or retirement plans. Financially they have nothing and I know of people in their 70's and 80's who were forced to look for jobs to sustain themselves.

Though Jehovah's Witnesses have made provisions to help other Witnesses who have suffered from natural disasters, they do not have any established charity organization nor do they support any others. This is because Jehovah's Witnesses are not permitted to contribute money or support charitable religious organizations as it would mean supporting "false religion."

Some believe that relocating their headquarters from Brooklyn, New York to Upstate New York had financial reasons. Their property in Brooklyn had an estimated value of one billion US Dollars or more. Furthermore they have been reducing the quantities of printed literature due to an online availability of their publications. The staff at the headquarters, Bethel Homes and other fulltime ministers is under the process of being reduced. As there is no published official financial information we are left with speculations.

Chapter 13
Doctrines

Here are some of the most important doctrines and beliefs of Jehovah's Witnesses.

Teachings about God, Jesus Christ and the Holy Spirit

Jehovah's Witnesses do not believe in the Trinity.

God's name is Jehovah. Only to Him, people may direct prayers in Jesus' name.

Jesus Christ is His only begotten son, having a pre-human existence (arch angel Michael).
In 1914 Jehovah appointed Jesus to rule as heavenly King. He will be the ruler during the Millennium and then return all power and authority to his father Jehovah.

One has to believe in Jesus and accept his ransom sacrifice in order to obtain forgiveness of sins and everlasting life. Jesus did not die on a cross, but was executed being nailed to a torture stake.

The Holy Spirit is not a person, but God's active force which he used to create the universe and inspired The Bible. He gives this Spirit to guide, help and bless his heavenly and earthly servants.

The Bible

God inspired 39 men to write all 66 books of The Bible, from Genesis to Revelation. It is the only written document revealing his will and purpose.

Soul and Death

Man does not have a soul, but he is a soul. When a person dies, the soul ceases to exist with all its thoughts and feelings.

God's Kingdom

God's Kingdom consists of Jesus Christ, the King and 144,000 faithful followers. These 144,000 heavenly "kings and priests" are His first 144,000 faithful followers "born again" by God's Spirit. Their resurrection to heavenly life began in 1919 and their number was complete in 1935. The Watchtower from May 1, 2007 modifies this by saying that God reserves the right to select some faithful Christians to be anointed after 1935.

Everlasting Life and Resurrection of the Dead

Faithful servants of God, and people in the past who never had an opportunity to believe in Jehovah, will receive a resurrection on earth during the Millennium rule of Jesus Christ. They will come back to life with a healthy human body and their former personality. They will have the opportunity to decide for Jehovah and for the prospects of everlasting life in a final test at the end of the Thousand-Year-Reign of Jesus Christ. They will never have to die again and will live forever on a Paradise Earth.

Death dissolves marriage. For many decades it was taught that people will not be able to marry again or have children after being resurrected. Currently the answer to the question of marriage and having children in the resurrection is left open.

At this point I would like to make a personal comment on the subject. Would the resurrection as it is taught by Jehovah's Witnesses really make people happy?

Using the example of my mother who passed away,

155

believing in being united with her beloved ones again in a resurrection I would say NO. First of all my resurrected mother would probably have to face the fact that her husband (my father) will not agree to live with her again. Furthermore she would have to accept that only one of her four children and two of her eight grandchildren live in paradise, the other ones being dead forever, according the understanding of Jehovah's Witnesses of who will get everlasting life and who not.

If her resurrected grandchild (my deceased son Manuel) would ask her where his beloved father is, she would have to answer: He deserved eternal death as he became an "apostate" writing even a book about dangerous religious thinking and a book asking questions to God.

I believe that it would be better for my mother and my son not to experience a resurrection from the dead as they would not like to live under those circumstances. ... And many more dramas would happen if there is a resurrection of the dead as Jehovah's Witnesses teach it.

Invisible Presence and Second Coming of Christ

In October of 1914 Jesus Christ was appointed to rule as heavenly King and His "invisible presence" (Greek: parousia) began. He cast Satan and his demons out of heaven and limited their activities to the earthly realm. The "last days" began and will end with the "Coming of Christ" in the "Great Tribulation." The "Great Tribulation" will begin with the destruction of all false religions, initiated by the United Nations (UNO), as God will have put this thought into their minds. It will continue with an unsuccessful attack on God's People by Satan, and end in Armageddon. In this battle of God, all governments of the earth and people who do not have God's protection will be destroyed by God's Kingdom. Then the Thousand-Year-Reign of Christ will begin. The surviving God's People will transform the earth into a paradise under Christ's supervision. They will have the prospect of everlasting life and live forever as human beings on earth.

The Last Supper

Jehovah's Witnesses commemorate Jesus' death on the 14th day of the Jewish month Nisan, usually the first full moon after the spring equinox, most often a day during Easter Week. They have a meeting after sunset, listening to a talk and then passing around bread and wine modeling the Last Supper. The bread is a symbol for Jesus' perfect human body and the wine represents his blood sacrificed for humankind. As these symbols are passed, only those who confess to belong to the 144,000 anointed follower of Christ are allowed to partake. Worldwide, 19,521 partakers of those symbols were counted in 2017. This number grows each year (2005 there were 8,524 partakers). In 2018 20,329,317 people attended the Memorial Service, revealing the potential of growth of the organization.

Angels, Satan and Demons

Jehovah created billions of angels. Satan and his Demons are apostate angels who were cast out to the vicinity of earth in 1914. The reason why God permits suffering and allows bad things to happen, are issues raised by Satan. He claimed, according to the Bible book of Job, that men would not remain faithful worshipers of God when experiencing bad things. God permits bad things to happen to answer these challenging issues. During the Millennium rule of Christ, Satan and his Demons will be imprisoned. Then, they will be permitted to leave their prison to test mankind; after which, they will be destroyed forever. All spiritualistic practices originate with Satan and his Demons.

Politics and other religions

Satan is the God and Ruler of this world. All political and religious organizations except for Jehovah's Witnesses are under Satan's influence and will get destroyed by God's Kingdom. This is the reason why Jehovah's Witnesses do not participate in political elections, do not accept political positions and do not become members or support military and religious organizations. Standing up during a national anthem or saluting the flag is considered to be idolatry. If there is conflict, they decide to obey God more than humans. They see themselves as citizens of a theocratic order under God's Kingdom.

The position of women and children

Men are encouraged to treat women and children lovingly and with respect.

For children, the perspective of everlasting life depends on their willingness to obey their parents.

The man is the "head of the woman."

Women are not allowed to take a responsible position in the congregation and cannot say a prayer in front of the congregation.

They are not permitted to pray in front of their families if the husband or a baptized son is present.

If there is no baptized man present, a woman may say a prayer in the meeting of the congregation while having her head covered.

Women are not allowed to give sermons or talks.

They can participate in congregation meetings, give comments after raising their hand or in the setting of an interview or a conversation on stage.

No part of the world

There is a warning that exists regarding the cultivation of any friendships with people who are not Jehovah's Witnesses and a caution to reduce social contacts with "people of the world" to a minimal necessity.

Considerable parts of talks and programs at assemblies are dedicated to warning against certain movies, books, TV shows, computer games, "worldly" parties, "harmful" music and "inappropriate" clothing and appearance.

There are constant admonishments against "worldly" university education and philosophy.

Marrying a non-Witness is never approved. No "judicial committee" will be called because of this; but a wedding ceremony in the Kingdom Hall and "privileges" in the congregation are always denied.

What Jehovah's Witnesses are not allowed to do

They never take part in customs or activities related to holidays that base their origin in politics, "false religion" and paganism, i.e. Christmas, Easter, birthdays, Valentine's Day, Thanksgiving or memorial days etc. They do not use or honor the cross, as it is identified as a pagan symbol.

They refuse to eat blood or blood products, i.e. in sausage or animals where the blood has not been shed after slaughtering them.

Jehovah's Witnesses do not accept medical treatment that involve receiving "principle components" of the blood, which are, according to their definition, Erythrocytes (red blood cells), Leukocytes (white blood cells), Thrombo-cytes (platelets) and Plasma.

The use, planting or selling of tobacco and non-medical drugs is prohibited; and getting drunk, condemned.

It is never permissible to gamble or play the lottery.

Abortion is considered murder, as well as contraceptives which prevent the fertilized egg cell to grow.

Masturbation, petting between people not married to each other, oral and anal sex, premarital and extramarital sex and love making between homosexuals is condemned.

The only reason which justifies divorce and the right to remarry is an act of sexual unfaithfulness of one partner. Even staying overnight alone with someone of the opposite sex or a homosexual who is not an immediate family member is considered evidence of adultery. Only the "innocent" one has the right to divorce the partner. If one gets a divorce because of a different reason than mentioned and remarries, he or she will get excommunicated for adultery. If one's spiritual or physical health is in danger one may separate but not remarry.

Greeting or having contact with an excommunicated Jehovah's Witness is not allowed. There is a warning not to read publications written by apostates.

Chapter 14
Life of a "typical" Jehovah's Witness

Life of a "typical Witness" is busy with attending religious services in the Kingdom Hall, evangelizing work and preparing for all these activities. Of course, leisure time activities, visiting friends and vacation times are also part of their lives. Naturally these are limited by a full schedule of religious activities.

Attending weekly and yearly religious services is not voluntarily. Hebrews 10:24, 25 is quoted to prove that it is God's command to attend religious meetings. The only accepted reasons for not attending are sickness, vacation or working shifts.

There are two weekly church services or "meetings":

One night they have "Our Christian Life and Ministry Meeting". The schedule and material is provided in a monthly *Our Christian Life and Ministry—Meeting*

Workbook (jw.org). It contains outlines of sample presentations for the ministry. This is a meeting where training to improve evangelizing methods, preaching activities and a Bible study program are scheduled.

During weekends, a 30 minute sermon is given by a local elder or guest speaker followed by a question and answer session conducted with an article from the current monthly Watchtower magazine.

It is expected that everyone comes prepared, has studied The Watchtower literature, and is up to date with the weekly Bible reading program. At the beginning and end of each meeting, a short prayer is offered by an assigned male Witness. During the meeting, three assigned songs taken from a Watchtower song book are sung.

There are short weekly meetings before groups of Publishers or Pioneers preach for several hours in assigned neighborhood territories.

On certain days one is assigned to participate in cleaning

of the Kingdom Hall.

Attendance at three yearly assemblies is expected.

It is expected that one comes to the meetings dressed with "appropriate" clothes, i.e. a dress or skirt for women, a suit or jacket with shirt and tie for men. There is encouragement to spend time visiting with the "brothers and sisters" before and after services.

In a Kingdom Hall there are no religious symbols and no altar. In the background of the stage, you can read the motto of the year. Rooms of a Kingdom Hall include different conference rooms, a library, a board with announcements and a table where one can obtain literature or audio/video products from The Watchtower Society. Monetary collections do not take place during the service, however, there are always boxes available for voluntary donations.

In an exemplary family of Jehovah's Witness, a weekly Bible study session is conducted with each of the children in addition to the weekly family session. At meal times the family reads a Bible text and a comment from the booklet "Examining the Scriptures Daily". Furthermore, there are assignments for personal Bible reading programs and one is expected to be prepared for these weekly meetings at the Kingdom Hall.

A Witness usually spends a couple of hours each week in evangelizing work from house to house, on the phone, online or on the streets with the Watchtower and Awake magazines and other publications.

Exemplary "elders" may be invited to participate in various additional opportunities to serve. This may include giving sermons in neighboring congregations, participating in a "Hospital Liaison Committee", working on a construction team for Kingdom Halls, joining a "Hospital Visiting Group", assisting in preparing assemblies or acting as a member of a "judicial committee."

Chapter 15

Are Jehovah's Witnesses a fundamentalist religion?

Here is a quotation from the Wikipedia Encyclopedia:

"Fundamentalism is the demand for a strict adherence to orthodox theological doctrines usually understood as a reaction against Modernist theology, primarily to promote continuity and accuracy. The term "fundamentalism" was originally coined by its supporters to describe five specific classic theological beliefs of Christianity, and that developed into a movement within the Protestant community of the United States in the early part of the 20th century, and that had its roots in the Fundamentalist–Modernist Controversy of that time. The term usually has a religious connotation indicating unwavering attachment to a set of irreducible beliefs. . . . The term can also refer specifically to the belief that one's religions texts are infallible and historically accurate, despite possible contradiction of these claims by modern scholarship."

Jehovah's Witnesses are not terrorists. They don't produce "suicide bombers", they are peaceful people who do not approve violence. People have found happiness, stability, a purpose in life, moral standards and a hope for the future in this "brotherhood."

But it is also true that people suffer physically, emotionally and spiritually because of religious fundamentalist thinking and authoritative structures of the organization of Jehovah's Witnesses. Due to some beliefs, a Witness can spend years of their lives unnecessarily in prison, lose their health or even their lives. Some suffer from the loss of family members, friends and material possessions and security. They give up the right to think for themselves and arrive at their own conclusions.

Jehovah's Witnesses are a fundamentalist thinking, authoritarian religious group that manipulates and controls the lives of their members. They claim to be the *only* religion blessed, accepted, approved and guided by God. They teach that you *have to be* a Jehovah's Witness to survive God's approaching "Judgment Day."

170

The Organization of Jehovah's Witnesses is a fundamentalist religion.

Made in the USA
Middletown, DE
30 October 2021